SOCIAL DETERMINANTS OF HEALTH SECTORAL BRIEFING SERIES 3

TRANSPORT (ROAD TRANSPORT): SHARED INTERESTS IN SUSTAINABLE OUTCOMES

World Health Organization

Acknowledgements
The Social Determinants of Health (SDH) *Sectoral Briefing Series* is being produced by WHO Headquarters in partnership with the Regional Office for the Western Pacific.

Transport: shared interests in sustainable outcomes was produced under the overall direction of Rüdiger Krech (Director, Ethics, Equity, Trade and Human Rights) in collaboration with Henk Bekedam (Director, Health Sector Development).

The publication was written by Daniel Albrecht, Gerardo Zamora, David Banister (University of Oxford), Nicole Valentine and Carlos Dora. Critical inputs related to concepts and research evidence were provided by Meleckidzedeck Khayesi, Anjana Bhushan and Elaine Fletcher. The principal editors were Daniel Albrecht, Nicole Valentine and Anjana Bhushan. Funding to assist in the preparation and production of the briefing was received from the Government of Brazil.

Valuable external peer review comments on drafts of the briefing were provided by Bernardo Baranda, David Behrens, Indu Bhushan and Dario Hidalgo.

Editorial production was managed by Daniel Albrecht. The paper was copy edited by Diana Hopkins.

WHO Library Cataloguing-in-Publication Data
Transport (road transport): shared interests in sustainable outcomes.

(Social determinants of health sectoral briefing series, 3)

1.Transportation. 2.Motor vehicles. 3.Accidents, Traffic - prevention and control. 4.Public policy. 5.Socioeconomic factors. 6.Policy making. I.World Health Organization. II.Series.

ISBN 978 92 4 150258 0 (NLM classification: WA 275)

Printed by the WHO Document Production Services, Geneva, Switzerland

Design and layout: Paprika-Annecy.

PREFACE

Public health is built on effective interventions in two broad domains: the biomedical domain that addresses diseases; and the social, economic and political domain that addresses the structural determinants of health. Effective health policy needs to tackle both domains. However, less rigorous and systematic attention has been paid to health issues in social, economic and political domains in recent decades.

Increasingly complex social, economic and political factors are affecting health and health policy-making. One area of complexity relates to health inequities. As emphasized by the WHO Commission on Social Determinants of Health, the social gradient in health is driven by policies in other sectors. Hence, looking at population well-being from the perspective of health and health equity rather than disease demands a new approach to intersectoral collaboration and an imperative to participate earlier in policy processes. Some of the new responsibilities for public health include:

- understanding the political agendas and administrative imperatives of other sectors;
- creating regular platforms for dialogue and problem solving with other sectors;
- working with other arms of government to achieve their goals and, in so doing, advancing health and well-being[1].

By providing information on other sectors' agendas and policy approaches, and their health impacts, and by illustrating areas for potential collaboration, the *Social Determinants of Health Sectoral Briefing Series* aims to encourage more systematic dialogue and problem solving, and more collaboration with other areas of government.

Examples of intersectoral action for health – current and historical – reveal that health practitioners are frequently perceived as ignoring other sectors' goals and challenges. This creates barriers to intersectoral work, limiting its sustainability and expansion. In order to avoid this perception, instead of starting from the goals of the health system (e.g. health, health equity, responsiveness, fairness in financial contributions), the *Social Determinants of Health Sectoral Briefing Series* focuses on the goals of other sectors. Rather than concentrating on traditional public health interventions (e.g. treatment, prevention, protection), the series use the goals of other sectors to orient its analyses and explore areas of mutual interest.

The target audience for the series is public health officers, who are not experts on determinants of health, but who have responsibilities for dealing with a broad range of development issues and partners. Each briefing will focus on a specific policy area, summarizing and synthesizing knowledge from key informants in health and other areas, as well as from the literature. They will present arguments, and highlight evidence of impacts and interventions, with special emphasis on health equity. They will make the case to health authorities for more proactive and systematic engagement with other sectors to ensure more responsive and cohesive governments that will meet broader societal aspirations for health, equity and human development.

Dr. Rüdiger Krech
Director
Department of Ethics, Equity, Trade and Human Rights
World Health Organization

1 WHO and Government of South Australia. *Adelaide Statement on Health in All Policies.* Adelaide, 2010.

THE TRANSPORT SECTOR (ROAD TRANSPORT)

Mutually reinforcing interests

Transport plays a critical role in societies; it facilitates the movement of people, goods and services, and contributes to economic and human development. There are different categorizations of transport modes, the most commonly identifiable in the literature are: road, rail, pipeline, inland waterway, sea and air. Of these, motorized road transport plays a critical role in the majority of countries, especially, private motor vehicles [2].

Motorized vehicles have provided and continue to provide enormous benefits to communities and countries around the world. One of the primary documented benefits associated with the growth in motorization is economic growth, which is associated with improved living standards (Banister, 2005). For many people, private motor vehicle transport is preferred to other options for reasons of convenience and comfort, in particular where public transport is unavailable or unreliable.

Yet the rising number of private motor vehicles is contributing to transport system inefficiencies and leading to decreased investments in public transport and non-motorized transport. The increased numbers of private motor vehicles on the roads is associated with several negative impacts (also known as 'external costs'), such as congestion, air and noise pollution, greenhouse gas (GHG) emissions, injuries and psychosocial impacts (Liu, 2005). While more concentrated in urban areas, these 'external costs' are also important for rural areas. They impact not only on population health but on the very sustainability of transport systems (Banister, 2005; Vasconcellos, 2001; Tiwari, 2005).

Thus, alternative patterns of development for transport systems are needed. Transport systems that are less reliant on motor vehicles, are designed to enhance public transport systems and take into account the needs of non-motorized users – with infrastructure for bicycles and pedestrians – are more sustainable. They improve health and promote economic and human development.

Global road transport trends

Since 1960, the global motor vehicle fleet has doubled every 15 years to reach 800 million in 2010. Currently, 70 per cent of the global fleet is in high-income countries (Schafer et al., 2009).

Yet, it is estimated that the total stock of vehicles will grow to at least 2 billion by 2050 and possibly much higher, depending especially on ownership trends in countries such as India and the People's Republic of China (IEA, 2009). Indeed, it is expected that the number of vehicles in these countries will surpass the number of vehicles in high-income countries by 2030 (Wright & Fulton, 2005). Vehicle usage is increasing while, in much of the world, public transit is decreasing. Figure 1 shows trends in the share of modes of public transport in four cities. The bars show baseline year values and comparative values for a specific point in time. The general trend in these cities is a loss in the share of modes of public transport. It is estimated that public transport is relinquishing a 0.2–1.4 per cent share annually (Wright & Fulton, 2005).

Figure 1. Trends in public transport mode share across four selected major cities

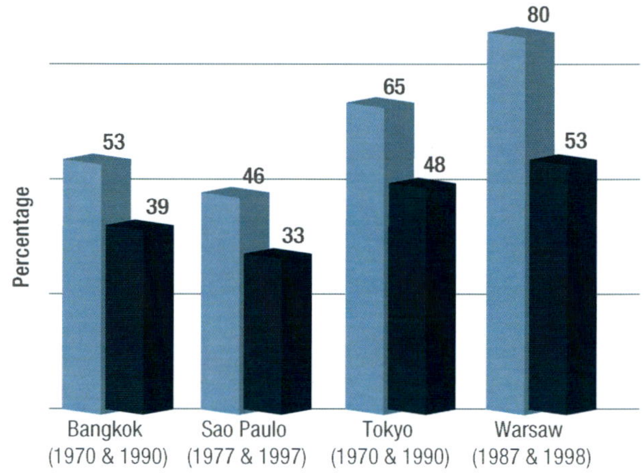

Source: Wright & Fulton (2005).

READER'S GUIDE

This briefing describes challenges facing transport policy-makers and authorities, how they address them, and areas for potential collaboration between health and transport. There are three sections.

1. Transport Sector Overview. This covers mutual public policy interests of transport and health; global trends in road transport; transport policy challenges from the perspective of the transport sector characterized as overarching 'goals' and situates these goals within a broad policy, economic, and stakeholder context.

2. Goals 1 to 5. The second part of the briefing allocates two to three pages to each goal, covering a more detailed description of policy approaches; health impacts and pathways; and examples of areas for joint work between health and transport.

3. Summary Messages. The briefing has been structured to permit those with limited time to obtain a well-rounded perspective of the topic by reading only sections one and three.

2 Private motor vehicles referred in this paper do not include two-wheelers, nor motor vehicles used to transport passengers (e.g. busses, taxis, etc). They are also referred to as Light-Duty Vehicles (LDV).

In low- and middle-income countries, where motorization is a relatively recent phenomenon, motorized transport is rapidly replacing traditional non-motorized transport modes such as walking and cycling. In spite of this, low- and middle-income countries' investments in road infrastructure have generally not kept up with the pace of motorization and do not usually take into account the needs of non-motorized transport users (e.g. pedestrians, cyclists). This trend is associated with high rates of road fatalities that are particularly harsh for low-income and vulnerable populations (WHO 2004; 2011a). Children are particularly affected. Indeed, globally road injuries are the second largest cause of mortality for the 5–14 age group, with 70 per cent of fatalities in low-income countries (WHO, 2009). It is estimated that the cost of traffic accidents amounts to US$ 518 billion, and represents between 1 per cent and 1.5 per cent of GDP in low- and middle-income countries, and 2 per cent of GDP in high-income countries (Jacobs et al., 2000; UNEP, 2011).

Overall, urban areas around the world are experiencing increasing congestion. This is causing higher transport costs and longer travel times, which often affect low-income groups the most. Congestion robs the European Union (EU) of 1 per cent of its entire gross domestic product (GDP). Across Europe, it is estimated that 2500 lives could be saved each year if emergency vehicles were not delayed on congested roads (TBC & IBM, 2009). In the United States, the cost of the time wasted on congested roads and extra fuel consumption is estimated at 0.7 per cent of GDP or around US$ 675 billion (FHWA, 2000). In Lima, Peru, it is estimated that on average a person spends four hours a day on congested roads resulting in lost productivity of around US$ 6.2 billion a year – equivalent to 10 per cent of the country's GDP (UNESCAP, UN-ECLAC & Urban Design Lab, 2010).

The expansion of road infrastructure to cope with the increased use of motorized vehicles is also affecting land availability and usage. Frequently, large tracts of land are divided into smaller plots limiting movement across formerly contiguous areas, affecting community life, social cohesion, ecosystems and health. Moreover, road infrastructure expansion impacts on land use affecting agricultural productivity and farming activities (Hunter, Farrington & Walton, 2001). Road expansion also favours infrastructure enlargement and overlooks the needs of low-income groups who are more likely to be short-distance commuters living in informal settlements (Dora & Philips M, 2000; Tiwari, 2003). Road expansion coupled with low density urban sprawl makes mobility dependent on cars, further limiting options for low-income, less-motorized communities.

Transport is also having an impact on climate change. While other sectors are progressing in reducing their contribution to green house gas emissions (e.g. housing, agriculture), the growth in motorization has increased emissions in the transport sector so that it is now the largest contributor to CO2 emissions (World Bank, 2010). Approximately 27 per cent of total emissions in member countries of the Organisation for Economic Co-operation and Development (OECD) come from transport and, of this, road transport accounts for approximately 80 per cent (OECD, 2002). Unfortunately, gains in cleaner vehicle technologies are offset by increasing numbers of vehicles (Banister, 2007; Schafer et al., 2009). At a local level, road networks also contribute to 'heat island effects' created by the absorption of radiation by asphalt pavements that warm cities. This is linked to fatalities among vulnerable groups such as elderly people and those with chronic conditions during extreme weather events like heat waves (O'Neill, Zanobetti & Schwartz, 2005).

In recent years, growing awareness of these negative impacts has galvanized some countries into adopting innovative approaches that examine the needs of all transport users (motorized and non-motorized) to improve coordination between transport, urban planning and housing policies. This reorientation has permitted the expansion of public transport systems (e.g. bus rapid transit) coupled with active transport options such as cycling and walking (e.g. Brazil, Canada, Chile, China, Colombia, Mexico and Nigeria). However, policy-makers acknowledge that more needs to be done in order to address the negative effects of transport and its sustainability. Taking into consideration these trends, the transport sector commonly identifies with the five policy goals listed in Table 1.

Table 1. A set of policy goals commonly addressed in the transport sector

	GOAL	DESCRIPTION
1	Economic development. Sustainable transport systems enhance economic development, while minimizing potential negative impacts.	Transport should support the efficient movement of people, goods and services to contribute to economic development and minimize the negative impacts associated in particular with congestion.
2	Safety. Sustainable transport systems improve safety.	Transport systems should be safe throughout the entire network, including roads, pedestrian zones and vehicles, and should be designed to avoid and reduce injuries and fatalities, and contribute to the health of local populations.
3	Accessibility. Transport systems ensure everyone can access transport services and facilities without barriers.	Transport systems should be designed to serve the needs of all people, addressing the barriers that prevent mobility, especially for disadvantaged groups.
4	Environmental sustainability. Transport systems promote environmentally sustainable transport options.	Transport should ensure mobility by adopting environmentally sound systems and modes.
5	Liveable communities and livelihoods. Sustainable transport systems promote mobility conducive to livelihood security and liveable communities.	Transport systems should contribute to social cohesion by addressing congestion; improving public transport systems and policies aimed at reducing car use; developing infrastructure for pedestrians and cyclists; and by encouraging social interaction and livelihood security.

Transport goals: towards sustainable mobility

A core assumption of emerging best practice in transport is that transport systems need to have long-run sustainability. For policy-makers, this means placing an increasing emphasis on the following three overarching principles:

(i) During planning and decision-making processes, policy-makers should adopt an equity approach and consider the needs of disadvantaged and vulnerable groups in societies, which are often overlooked.

(ii) Although motorized vehicles (including private motor vehicles) are not negative per se, it is essential to explore potential alternative transport technologies that could cater to the needs of different users (e.g. provide transport alternatives for short-distance trips in both urban and rural areas).

(iii) Integrated policy-making processes need to consider the mandates, goals and interests of the different policy stakeholders beyond transport, including health, urban planning and environment in order to develop more sustainable transport systems.

Policy perspectives

The economic perspective. Transport systems contribute to economic activity and economic development. While different economies have different levels of mobility, in general, enhanced mobility means more opportunities for further economic development.

At the macro level, the transport sector's contribution to the economy can be measured in different terms: (i) how the provision of transport facilitates the movement of goods and services to markets, and the process of industrialization and economic growth; (ii) the direct valuation of the transport of goods and services; (iii) the direct contribution of industry to employment; and (iv) how patterns of investment are influenced across sectors.

(i) Industrialization and economic growth. Historically, economic growth measured by growth in GDP has been coupled with growth in demand for freight and passenger traffic (Banister, 2005). Due to external costs, including congestion and pollution, which have simultaneously arisen, the debate among transport policy-makers now is how to de-couple economic growth and transport intensity and reduce the 'transport intensity' of economic activities. For example, European Union de-coupling strategies have focused on raising the occupancy of the vehicle fleet, reducing vehicle kilometres, and by encouraging modal shift (e.g. facilitating the use of a combination of cycling and public transport to reach workplaces) (Banister, 2005).

(ii) Production of goods and services across transport-related sub-sectors. This includes services and 'equipment manufacturing' and other related industries (e.g. automotive repair, service stations, car dealers, and highway construction and toll roads). In many developed countries, transport accounts between 6 per cent and 12 per cent of GDP (Rodrigue, 2008). In the United Kingdom and France, the transport sector accounts on average for about 7 per cent of GDP (UNECE 2001).

(iii) Employment. In the United States in 2002, the transport and related sector's jobs' share of the total labour force was 15.6 per cent. In the United States alone, the automotive industry contributes 3.3 per cent to GDP and provides work, directly or indirectly, to 10 per cent of the labour force (McAliden et al., 2003).

(iv) Investment patterns. The transport sector is also a key driver of investment decisions in other sectors. For example, transport infrastructure investments need to be spatially synchronized with investments in other sectors such as regional development, agriculture, tourism and housing. Energy prospecting is also driven by predictions of transport trends.

At the micro-level, transport is a cost borne by many businesses and households. Transport costs can increase or decrease business competitiveness or even threaten their viability. Experts estimate transport expenditure accounts for around 4 per cent of unit output costs in manufacturing, with this figure being greater for some service industries, such as tourism (Rodrigue, 2008). Transport costs have a considerable impact on households' disposable incomes. High transport costs for disadvantaged groups can adversely affect their access to schools, social and health services, and prevent their full participation in society. On average, transport costs account for between 10 per cent and 15 per cent of household expenditure and these averages are often higher for lower income groups (Lipman 2006; Rice 2004; STPP 2003). In Lima, Peru (population 10 million), it was recently estimated that transport costs for the poorest households accounted for around 40 per cent of the household expenditure (Bielich, 2010).

Stakeholders in the transport sector. Governments set strategic directions for the development of transport systems, raise taxes from vehicle licence fees, fund transport infrastructure projects, and promote and regulate the sector with regard to safety standards and specific transport options (e.g. motor vehicles, public transport and non-motorized active transport). Local governments and their urban planning departments are key actors. They are involved in the implementation of national policies and regulations, and in identifying the need for new road networks and road maintenance, as well as in the development of other public transport options. Police authorities at national and local levels play an important role in implementing legislation aimed at traffic calming[3] or regular vehicle maintenance (e.g. road worthiness tests). Regulations related to vehicle and emissions standards, or licensing of drivers or vehicles may empower quasi-independent boards to monitor compliance.

Providers of public transport vary according to countries. In general, they are either public corporations, regulated private providers or, as in many low- and middle-income countries, informal transport operators. Drivers are another important stakeholder group. Many times their terms of employment affect their ability to influence their working conditions in the transport sector. Very often this is translated into drivers having to work long hours with no regular pauses or time to rest. In Lima, Peru in average a public transport driver works around 14 hours per day, six days per week (Bielich, 2010). Added to other factors, such as congestion and lack of enforcement, very often this increases road injuries and fatalities.

3 Intended to slow or reduce motor-vehicle traffic in order to improve residents' living conditions as well as improve safety for pedestrians and cyclists.

Private sector construction firms commonly contract with transport authorities to implement infrastructure projects. International lending organizations such as the World Bank, regional development banks and some bilateral donors play an important role in financing the construction of transport infrastructure. Private industries, ranging from vehicle manufacturers to spare parts wholesalers and energy companies, have an important economic role in the provision of transport products and services as well as in some cases an active lobbying role for more vehicle infrastructure.

The public make decisions about their mobility based on the demands and needs of their daily lives, and the cost and convenience of different transport options. They may belong to associations that represent the interests of vehicle owners, but only a few associations represent the interests of non-motorized or public transport users. In general, the public's influence on decision-making related to transport is weak, in contrast to more concentrated commercial interests. However, at the local level they often have opportunities to exercise their voice, for example, during environmental impact assessments.

Sustainable transport is feasible. The trends described before can change. Sustainable transport requires modifications to how countries and cities are developed. This involves making changes to current policies that very often favour motorization, and to advances in technology and transport management. It does not necessarily mean higher costs to the economy. The International Energy Agency projected a trend scenario in which, if current conditions remain, by 2050 global production of additional motorized light duty vehicles (LDVs) would amount to US$ 150 billion with an additional cost of US$ 150 billion for fuel (IEA, 2010). If these resources were, at least partially, reallocated to mix-use and dense urban development, to infrastructure for walking, cycling and public transport, and to cleaner technologies, progress towards sustainable transport could be advanced.

Recent studies show that by using available resources and implementing these changes, it would be possible to achieve a 68 per cent reduction in GHG emissions (8.4 gigatonnes of CO_2) on these projected trends (Bailey, Mokhtarian & Little, 2008). This reallocation would yield employment gains of around 10 per cent. These estimations do not include impacts on accessibility and health, which are estimated to be high when considering the reduction in GHG (UNEP, 2011). Equally important is the fact that this will only be possible if government sectors work in a more coordinated and integrated way on policy formulation and governance reform. The health sector in particular can actively explore ways to engage with the transport sector to identify areas where mutual gains can be pursued.

SCOPE AND LIMITATIONS

The bulk of the burden of disease and the major causes of health inequities in all countries arise from the conditions in which people are born, grow, live, work and age. These conditions are known as social determinants of health – encompassing the social, economic, political, cultural and environmental determinants of health. The most important determinants are those that produce stratification in societies, namely structural determinants, such as the distribution of income, discrimination (e.g. on the basis of gender, class, ethnicity, disability or sexual orientation), and political and governance structures that reinforce inequalities in economic power. Discrepancies in social position arising from these mechanisms shape individual health status and outcomes through their impact on intermediary determinants such as living conditions, psychosocial factors and the health system.

Recognizing this spectrum of determinants, this briefing takes a national perspective, but makes reference to implementation at sub-national levels of government. The transport sector covers a wide range of transport modes. This first briefing focuses on road transport and motorization and especially on the growth of private motor vehicles. While contexts and governmental structures differ, many actions to address transport challenges occur at the local level, and also involve urban planning and land use authorities.

The scope of challenges and interventions described here specifically exclude, for reasons of space, detailed examination of private commercial interests.

GOAL 1. SUSTAINABLE TRANSPORT SYSTEMS ENHANCE ECONOMIC DEVELOPMENT, WHILE MINIMIZING POTENTIAL NEGATIVE IMPACTS

TRANSPORT SHOULD SUPPORT THE EFFICIENT MOVEMENT OF PEOPLE, GOODS AND SERVICES TO CONTRIBUTE TO ECONOMIC DEVELOPMENT AND MINIMIZE THE NEGATIVE IMPACTS ASSOCIATED IN PARTICULAR WITH CONGESTION.

Transport challenges and responses

Transport is a pillar of most economies, ensuring the movement of people, goods and services. It enables the economic specialization of labour and capital, leading to economic development. Yet, in facilitating economic activity, the dominance of motorized vehicles has given rise to negative impacts for economies and societies (Banister, 2005). These impacts mostly affect the poor, thereby limiting the sector's contribution to *inclusive* economic growth. The rapid expansion of motorized transport without due consideration of its negative impacts has been characterized as resulting in short-term gains for economic growth, that will be undermined in the future (DOT, 2006). Policy-makers, therefore, face the challenge of developing transport systems that can contribute to economic growth in the longer run, which means minimizing the potential negative impacts of the options chosen (Hoyle and Smith, 2001).

Congestion costs to businesses go beyond the mere vehicle and driver costs of delay. They include increased inventory costs, logistics costs, reliability costs, last-minute processing costs, and reductions in market areas for workers, customers and deliveries. Besides, congestion increases travel times and costs for business and consumers. Many hours are lost, reducing the quality of life of the population and especially the lower income groups who frequently live on the outskirts of cities in most developing countries. It makes public transport systems more expensive to operate, drives up fares, limits mobility and increases food prices, hitting low-income groups particularly hard. The expansion of road infrastructure eliminates public recreational spaces, pedestrian ways and green areas. Air pollution, deforestation and green house emissions (CO2) are other important areas that reduce the quality of environmental resources and impact on health expenditures (Banister, 2005; Holm-Hadulla, 2006).

It is transport policy-makers' view that it is possible to balance economic growth imperatives in the short- and long-term with other social impacts. A reorientation of transport policy design focusing on *people* and not *vehicles*, and specifically on the needs of all users (balancing motorized and non-motorized users) is a key underlying approach to achieving this (Appleyard 1981; Vasconcellos, 2004).

Balancing these different goals within 'sustainable transport systems' successfully requires *joint transport, housing and urban sectors policy formulation and planning.* This approach improves the ability of transport policy-makers to develop policies that anticipate the diverse impacts of transport policies and to avoid the negative ones (Kahlmeier et al., 2011). Within this framework, extending public transport – network coverage, service frequency, comfort and convenience, and physical accessibility to users – is an important policy priority. Other policy interventions to accompany these measures may include financial and regulatory measures, disincentives for private vehicle use and ownership aimed at reducing congestion, and improving travel times and traffic flows (e.g. congestion taxes, peak traffic flow rules, car-sharing lanes and reducing parking spaces or making them more expensive).

Examples of health impacts and pathways

Health impacts related to transport are linked to the different goals discussed in this document (e.g. road safety, pollution-related diseases). In this section, we explore some impacts related to the goal of supporting economic development. Each of the subsequent sections will focus on different types of health impacts associated with the other goals.

Increasing motorization and unhealthy living conditions. People are walking less and less in all countries regardless of income level, as motorization becomes the dominant means of transport. A study in Brazil of 385 people from low-income groups found that the lack of green leisure areas, reduced pedestrian ways, increased motorization, and the expansion of road infrastructure put up barriers for non-motorized road users and was associated with the decrease in walking, especially among women (Salvador, Reis & Florindo, 2010). Lack of physical activity, coupled with other risk factors, such as unhealthy diets, tobacco consumption and poor mental health, are leading to an obesity epidemic and a rise in the prevalence of non-communicable diseases (WHO, 1997; 2011b). Health policy makers in Scandinavian countries have a long history of promoting active commuting through transport and education policies. For example, in Sweden, obesity prevalence rates are among the lowest for high-income countries. Some of this is attributed to their vigorous promotion of active transport policies (Bassett et al., 2008; Lindberg, 2007). For children in particular, from all socioeconomic groups, active transport is feasible. Most children live close to their schools and attend public schools. A study in 2011 reported that between 45 per cent and 68 per cent of school children sampled were using active commuting (Johansson, Hasselberg & Laflamme, 2011). A recent systematic review commissioned by WHO (2010) recommends design and land use policies and practices that support physical activity in urban areas to reverse these trends.

Consumers and increased food costs. Transport costs affect the patterns of food production and food availability. Most transport systems rely on oil. Consequently, increases in fuel costs impact on food costs, reducing low-income groups' ability to afford healthy food, which in turn has an impact on their nutritional status (Dubowitz et al., 2008). According to the International Fund for Agricultural Development (IFAD), oil and food prices are highly correlated (IFAD, 2008). The Work Bank's Food Price Monitor estimates that since 2010 the number of people in extreme poverty has risen by 44 million in low- and middle-income countries, which it directly links to hikes in food prices (World Bank, 2011).

Transport and sexually transmitted infections. In many countries the growth of road networks boost economic growth but also impact on the spread of infections. The HIV epidemic tends to move along roads. Truck drivers, road construction workers and workers in a variety of services along roads (e.g. restaurant workers, mechanics, filling station employees and lodge owners) are at an increased risk for HIV (World Bank, 2009). Several surveys in India and Nepal show that the number of truckers that visit sex workers range from 25 per cent to 80 per cent. Those most vulnerable to HIV during road construction are skilled male workers (e.g. machine operators, drivers, supervisors, managers and engineers) and young rural women who often move close to construction sites. Local labourers are at less risk because they are usually drawn from local communities and go back to their families regularly (Asian Development Bank, 2009). Migrant road workers who are away from their social networks and families are exposed to HIV and other sexually transmitted infections. In western Nepal, a large number of new infections among women in remote villages were linked to the fact that their husbands were migrant road workers (World Bank, 2009). Changes in HIV/AIDS prevalence are documented along truck routes in all regions including countries like Brazil and many sub-Saharan Africa countries (Lacerda et al., 1997; Lemey et al., 2003). In Brazil, India and Zambia truck drivers are one of the most at risk populations. Data from India suggest that transport sector workers are twice as likely to become infected with HIV as other workers (World Bank, 2009). Furthermore, new roads bring more truck drivers who are often missed by HIV interventions.

What can both sectors do together?

Facilitate collaborative policy-making processes. Recent sustainable transport initiatives focus on joint planning and policy formulation processes. For example, the Transport, Health and Environment Pan-European Programme (THE PEP), an initiative of the WHO European Office and the United Nations Economic Commission for Europe (UNECE), is a coordinating mechanism for sustainable transport policies. It promotes a common policy framework for ministries of transport, health and the environment, whereby they set policy priorities and harmonize their mandates thus opening a channel for dialogue. The Transport, Health and Environment Pan-European Programme encourages countries to invest in environment- and health-friendly transport systems and healthy mobility systems for both users and non-users of motor vehicles. It promotes systems to reduce greenhouse gases and pollutants. It has created a platform for discussion and agenda setting where the goals and interests of the different sectors are considered. As outlined in the next paragraph, this mechanism has allowed for the production of technical materials that contribute to better and healthier transport systems enabling economic growth whilst avoiding the negative equity impacts. Stakeholders see an open channel for policy dialogue as critical in exploring policy responses that integrate the views of different actors. This channel questions traditional silo cultures that prevent dialogue across sectors.

Box 1. SOCIAL DETERMINANTS AND EQUITY FOCUS

Due to its expected high economic growth in the coming 20 years, China is considered the most important future market for new cars. The motorization rate (number of cars/1000 population) in 2005 in China was 15.8. It is predicted that by 2050 this rate will be 411.6 (a 28-fold increase). China will have a total share of 20 per cent of the global car fleet (Chamon, Mauro & Okawa, 2008).

Economic growth will increase the rate of motorization in China, which will very likely increase transport external costs. Some lessons can be drawn from current highly motorized countries that can inform future policies in China. Using a sample of 15 cities in the United States (10) and in Australia and New Zealand (five in both countries), Kenworthy and Townsend (2002) found the differences presented in Table 2.

Table 2. Selected transport indicators in 15 major cities in Australia and New Zealand, and the United States

SELECTED INDICATORS	AUSTRALIA & NEW ZEALAND	UNITED STATES
Urban density persons/hectare	15	15
Private car share of total transportation needs (percentage)	79	89
Available kms/per capita of public transport service	3628	1557
Proportion of jobs in CBD (percentage)	15	9
Deaths/100 000 people	8.6	11.5
Total emissions per capita (CO, SO2, VHC, NOx) kg/person	189	265

Source: Kenworthy & Townsend, 2002.

Although the majority of the cities studied in the three countries suffer from the negative impacts of mass motorization, some differences in their urban and transport policies can provide lessons for decision makers. The cities studied took diverse paths with different impacts on external costs. The availability of public transport and opportunities for non-motorized transport contributed to a reduction in both the number of fatalities and pollution levels in the cities studied in Australia and New Zealand. Also, the coordinated work of transport, urban planners and local authorities led to more centralized cities in Australia and New Zealand, which was associated with more people working in central areas (Core Business Districts – CBD). This lowered private car usage and led to an increase in the use of public transport. These experiences can be important lessons when building sustainable transport systems that enhance mobility and prevent negative impacts on social determinants of health.

Supporting assessment of policy options. Collaborative policy-making processes already described often create platforms of collaboration that allow the health sector to support transport authorities in assessing policy options. In recent years, the WHO Regional Office for Europe and its partners have contributed to sustainable transport policies by supporting authorities in their assessment of the role of physical activity, and safe walking and cycling. Several guidelines and tools for transport authorities to quantify the health effects of these activities have been prepared. Other technical materials have been prepared for transport planners to conduct economic assessments of cycling. These materials complement existing transport tools for economic valuations. In Austria, Sweden, New Zealand, the United Kingdom and the United States, these tools are used to improve transport systems and to facilitate movement of motorized and non-motorized users (WHO-EURO, 2007). In other European countries, the health sector provides transport authorities with evidence on the effects of pollution, noise and physical inactivity on children's health, and supports them in carrying out economic valuation assessments (Kahlmeier, 2011). These are some examples of potential areas of collaboration that national authorities could explore in order to contribute to the achievement of mutual goals.

Transport, economic growth and health. Rural transport is an area where investment is often overlooked. Estimates suggest that the population of rural Bangladesh uses 13 per cent of the roads in the rainy season, due to their being cut off from markets and social services by flooding. In 1991, the city of Dhaka and transport, health, sanitation and education authorities launched a project to make roads connected to the city accessible all year round in rural areas. The project focused on selected market places providing them with better access, water supply facilities, and sanitation and health services. This initiative resulted in a substantial reduction in transport costs and travel times. Furthermore, increased market activity coupled with enhanced agricultural production and food availability was fundamental in improving health and nutrition among the people that benefited from the initiative; school attendance improved as did people's access to health services (Holm-Hadulla, 2006). This case demonstrates that when planning social development interventions, health authorities can support local transport authorities by assessing proposed initiatives, backing decision-making processes and monitoring the health impacts in order to achieve common goals that promote economic growth, inclusion and better health.

Road tolls can reduce congestion and improve health. Since 1996, the Seoul Metropolitan Government charges a KRW 2000 (approximately US$ 1.70) congestion toll for private vehicles carrying up to two persons as they pass through specific sectors in the city. This initiative has reduced fuel consumption, emissions and noise (Shon, 2000; Son & Hwang, 2001). Both the health and transport sectors identified the impacts of these measures and their health gains. Moreover, in Seoul, car-free days have been useful in decreasing traffic volumes by 7 per cent and in reducing emissions by 12 per cent (Nurul, 2009). These interventions reduce the percentage of hospitalizations due to respiratory diseases and injuries (Cho et al., 2000; D'Amato, 2010); and increase social interaction by providing local residents and pedestrians with more recreational spaces (WHO, 2007a; Khayesi, Majoro & Johnson, 2010).

Reducing the negative health impacts of road infrastructure expansion. The health sector can collaborate with transport authorities in the planning, construction and operation of road infrastructure projects to prevent and address diverse health issues and risk factors. A review of initiatives to reduce exposure to HIV in road construction projects undertaken in 5 Asian countries (Cambodia, India, Papua New Guinea, People's Republic of China, and Tajikistan) showed several areas of potential collaboration that the health sector could explore (Asian Development Bank, 2009). Although the review focused on HIV, collaboration can also be explored to address other health issues common in infrastructure projects, such as occupational health, other infectious diseases and health promotion.

Activities can be implemented during pre-construction phases, for example, in order to include in project bidding documents responsibilities that offer or support the health sector's voluntary case detection services at work sites (HIV, TB and other diseases); adopt referral mechanisms to health-care facilities, provide training for emergency care, disseminate information on common health- related issues in work places; and monitor the adoption of standards that ensure that the infrastructure built can be used by everyone specially those with limited mobility (e.g. adopting universal design principles, see more in Goal 3). Equally important is the fact that the health sector can commission or directly undertake assessments of potential health impacts of infrastructure projects and anticipate, prevent or mitigate their negative impacts. The health sector can explore how projects could increase the vulnerability of specific groups. In pre-construction phases, health practitioners can also support and facilitate community consultations to assess people's needs, particularly involving vulnerable or excluded groups (e.g. sex workers).

During construction phases, health authorities can work with transport authorities, road infrastructure contractors and community groups on health promotion interventions for the prevention of occupational hazards, and other interventions to prevent and provide first care for HIV, tuberculosis, other transmissible diseases, workplace injuries, or exposure to toxic agents. The health sector can also contribute to the implementation of social marketing campaigns to address common risk factors affecting construction workers. Whenever possible, health practitioners can monitor and promote the employment of specific groups (e.g. re-employment of those recovering from workplace injuries).

During post-construction phases, several common initiatives can include the joint assessment of risk factors and diseases affecting road users, including truck drivers and mobile road maintenance workers, such as HIV and other infectious diseases, and the implementation of capacity building activities to prevent and manage diseases (Lacerda et al., 1997; Jabbari et al., 2010; Diallo et al., 2011). During construction or post-construction phases, health authorities can support vocational training and skills improvement activities for communities or groups that could have been affected by these projects. Given the impact that infrastructure projects often have on local communities, in implementing all these activities, the health sector can explore the possibility of establishing coordinating mechanisms to improve collaboration between all relevant stakeholders, including the health, transportation, infrastructure and law enforcement sectors, builders, community groups or NGOs.

Recommended reading

1. WHO-EURO (2007). *Economic assessment of transport infrastructure and policies.* Copenhagen, WHO Regional Office for Europe.
2. WHO-EURO (2000). *Transport, environment and health.* Copenhagen, WHO Regional Office for Europe (European Series No. 89).
3. Kahlmeier S et al. (2010). «Health in All Policies" in practice: guidance and tools to quantifying the health effects of cycling and walking. *Journal of Physical Activity and Health*, 7(Suppl. 1):S120–S125.
4. Vasconcellos E (2010). *Espacio medio ambiente y equidad* [Space, environment and equity]. Bogota, Corporacion Andina de Fomento.

Useful links

The PEP Clearing House – Transport, Health, and Environment Pan-European Programme implemented by WHO and UNECE. It provides information on transport, health and environmental sectors, and contains resources for decision-makers: http://www.thepep.org/CHWebsite/

Institute for Transportation and Development Policy (ITDP). Non-profit organization promoting sustainable and equitable transportation policies and projects worldwide. It advices national and local governments and implements partnerships and programmes for transport emissions reduction, protection of the environment, economic opportunities, and improvement of the quality of urban life: http://www.itdp.org/

Transport Research Board (TRB). Division of the National Research Council of the United States. It serves as an independent advisor to the federal government on scientific and technical questions on transport matters. It conducts and funds research and promotes information exchange: http://www.trb.org

GOAL 2. SUSTAINABLE TRANSPORT SYSTEMS IMPROVE SAFETY

TRANSPORT SYSTEMS SHOULD BE SAFE THROUGHOUT THE ENTIRE NETWORK, INCLUDING ROADS, PEDESTRIAN ZONES AND VEHICLES, AND SHOULD BE DESIGNED TO AVOID AND REDUCE INJURIES AND FATALITIES, AND CONTRIBUTE TO THE HEALTH OF LOCAL POPULATIONS.

Transport challenges and responses

Globally, 3500 people die daily on roads (1.2 million in 2009). Almost 90 per cent of fatalities occur in low- and middle- income countries, which only have 45 per cent of the global car fleet (WHO, 2009). This mortality is linked to the fact that motor vehicles in most LMI countries share the roads with light two- or three-wheeled vehicles, bicycles and pedestrians. While in high-income countries fatalities and injuries are mostly related to crashes and often affect drivers and passengers, in LMI the most affected are pedestrians and non-motorized road users (WHO, 2009). Almost 50 million people suffer road injuries every year (WHO, 2004). The costs of injuries for LMI countries is calculated at US$ 520 billion, approximately 1–3 per cent of countries' Gross Domestic Product (GDP) and more than the total amount of development aid for these countries (WHO, 2004; 2009).

As of 2009, road injuries were the tenth global leading cause of death for all ages (WHO, 2009). If the trends continue, it will move to sixth place by 2020 (Jacobs, Aeron-Thomas & Astrop, 2000). There is likely to be a growth in injuries in LMI countries. Lives lost and injuries will impact on economies, health systems and population health, and especially on the poor, who are the most vulnerable road users (Tiwari, 2011). Motorization has also increased insecurity: local communities are becoming less attractive for social interaction due to increased traffic and injuries (Vasconcellos E et al, 2010; Banister & Woodcock, 2011). The challenge for policy-makers is twofold: to increase safety for all users; and to address the unequal burden of road morbidity and mortality.

Thus far, advances in industry safety interventions have been mostly car-oriented; this has saved the lives of drivers but has not improved the safety of non-motorized users (Tiwari 2006; 2011). A critical feature of transport policy in this area is, therefore, to develop road safety initiatives for non-motorized users. Although not well organized, they constitute by far the largest groups of all stakeholders (Anand & Tiwari, 2006).

Road safety policies and interventions usually require active collaboration across transport, health, education, police and security sectors (EC, 2006). A key policy and practice challenge, therefore, is to foster good intersectoral working relationships and associated allocations of human and financial resources to act effectively together (WHO, 2009). Important road safety interventions include:

- infrastructure safety regulations (e.g. road construction standards, maintenance conditions and assessments);
- vehicle maintenance conditions and safety standards;
- drivers' training and tests, speed management, road users issues (e.g. helmets and seatbelt use, airbags, child restraints);
- alcohol/drugs consumption and risk-taking behaviours (WHO, 2004).

Safety considerations focusing on non-motorized users include:

- regulating sidewalks, traffic lights and signals;
- transit users' standards (e.g. public vehicles standards, commuting spaces, stops, information systems);
- other active users' standards (e.g. regulating bicycle lanes, lights and reflective bands);
- Safety awareness campaigns.

Examples of health impacts and pathways

The highest cause of death for young adults. Although road injuries are the tenth cause of mortality with 1.21 million deaths in 2010, it is the first for the 15–29 age group (WHO, 2009; 2011a). Even in countries where the share of 15–29 age groups has decreased because of ageing, the per capita fatality rate continues to be greater than in older groups, as is the case in Australia (Saffron, 2001).

Increasing demands on the health systems. Road accidents injure 50 million people a year, often causing permanent disabilities (WHO, 2004). Lack of trained expertise in trauma care often leads to permanent injury or death (WHO, 2004; 2009). A study in Ghana of 11 rural hospitals receiving large numbers of road injuries found that all these facilities were staffed by practitioners who had no trauma training (WHO, 2009). Demand for trauma services in resource-constrained environments also detracts medical attention from other categories of important hospital care, such as complicated deliveries.

Equity, pedestrians and mortality. Road mortality is unequally distributed among road users. In low-income countries, mortality among pedestrians and passengers is more likely to occur among low-income groups (Nantulya & Reich, 2003; Tiwari, 2005). In Kenya, 70 per cent of deaths due to road injuries are among pedestrians, 16 per cent are passengers and 8 per cent are drivers (WHO, 2009). Fatality rates in children in low- and middle-income regions are six times the rates in high-income countries (WHO, 2004; 2009).

Pedestrian safety. Research involving a sample of 667 working women in New Delhi, India, found that pedestrians and bus transit users are the most affected by unsafeness, which was characterized by a lack of footpaths and pedestrian crossings, the poor location of bus shelters and the high steps of public buses. Inadequate street lighting and poor design of bus stops also contributed to sexual harassment and gender violence (Anand & Tiwari, 2006).

Box 2. SOCIAL DETERMINANTS AND EQUITY FOCUS

Road traffic injuries are an important public health problem at global, regional and national levels. Despite comprising 48 per cent of all vehicles registered worldwide, low and middle income countries account 91 per cent of all road traffic deaths (Figure 2). Middle income countries present an imbalance, too. Around 75 per cent of road traffic deaths are among men and mostly those in economically active age ranges. Investments in transport safety become critical to reach the MDGs.

Figure 2. Road traffic deaths and registered vehicles by country income group, 2009

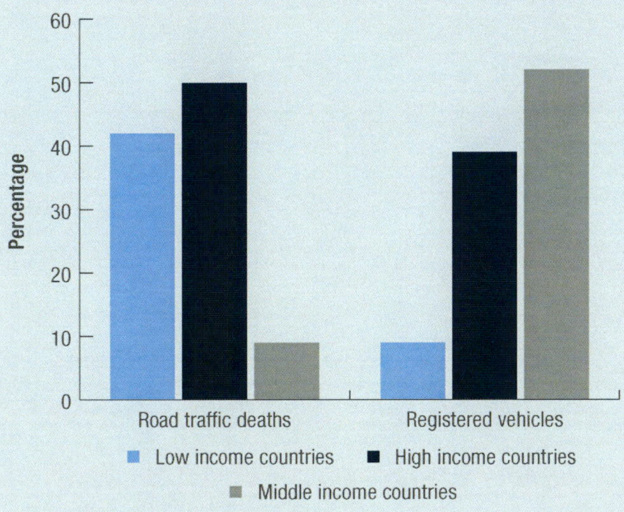

Source: WHO (2009).

What can both sectors do together?

Law enforcement reduces injuries and mortality. In Viet Nam, the wearing of motorcycle helmets became mandatory for all users of motorized two-wheelers in 2007 resulting in a 50 per cent drop in serious injuries for two-wheel vehicle drivers. National health authorities and WHO collaborated with transport authorities to introduce this new law. They carried out extensive advocacy work and put forward evidence-based policy directions to encourage policy-makers to adopt the legislation. Subsequent evaluation studies have found that helmets decreased the severity of injuries among motorcyclists by about 70 per cent and the likelihood of death by 40 per cent (GRSP, 2010).

A 2003 study in 15 European countries found that better enforcement could have avoided 5800 fatalities per year due to speeding, 4300 fatalities due to not wearing seat belts and 3800 fatalities from drink driving. In terms of injuries, 680 000 yearly injuries could have been avoided (ICF, 2003; European Commission, 2006). In France, the introduction of a set of law enforcement measures (e.g. speed limits, driving licence penalty points schemes, obligatory safety devices for drivers and passengers), which were coupled with broader campaigns and increased policing, reduced fatalities from 2996 in 1996 to 1576 in 2008. In Spain, over the same period, deaths fell from 2054 to 1129 (ERSO, 2010). These reductions in injury and mortality have had a great impact on health-care resources.

Promoting road safety measures. The health sector can work with transport authorities in the adoption and enforcement of regulations, and monitoring on compliance, as well as awareness campaigns related to the mandatory use of seat belts, child restraints, mandatory insurance regimes and other measures that can prevent road injuries. It can help transport to promote safer behaviours by supporting evidence-based policies. The two sectors can work together in assessing the economic impact of saved lives and saved health costs on national economies as a way of promoting awareness and political commitment to better road safety.

Assessing drivers' health and supporting graduated drivers' licensing. Beginner drivers of all ages lack both driving skills and experience in recognizing potential dangers. Studies show that newly licensed young drivers' immaturity and limited driving experience result in high accident rates (WHO-EURO, 2000; WHO 2004, 2009). This is true for older beginners as well (WHO, 2009). Graduated drivers' licensing systems address these risks with a coordinated action of health assessments and driving tests, informed by health practitioners. Graduated driver licensing has proved effective in reducing road accidents. Peer-reviewed evaluations by both health and transport professionals on the effectiveness of such schemes in Canada, New Zealand and the United States report reductions in the number of crashes caused by new drivers in the range of 9–43 per cent (WHO, 2009).

Supporting data gathering on injuries and mortality. In many countries, data collection on road safety is poor as it entails the coordination of transport and health actors to record cases of road injures. However, both sectors can collaborate in designing surveillance systems, as shown in community surveys conducted in Ghana, India and Viet Nam, which required the methodological expertise that was provided by health authorities. Guidelines providing a methodology for conducting these surveys are being developed by WHO for the health and transport sectors (WHO, 2009).

Even in large metropolises of developed countries, such as New York City, the United States, the monitoring of the impact of transport policy is informed by data from the health sector. The New York City Department of Health and Mental Hygiene prepares mortality and morbidity data related to road and transport causes and contributes to evaluation and policy decision-making processes. This makes possible to evaluate the success of transport initiatives to increase cycling lanes and spaces for people to walk. As a result, traffic fatalities have declined in New York City by about 30 per cent since 2000. Pedestrian deaths, which make up the largest proportion of traffic deaths, have declined by 59 per cent since 1990 (366 in 1990 vs. 151 in 2010) (NYC-VS, 2011).

Identifying opportunities for traffic calming. Speeding is a serious problem in many African countries. Ghana has road fatality rates that are 30–40 times greater than those in industrialized countries

(Afukaar et al., 2003). In order to address this trend, health, transport and law enforcement actors devised a strategy to increase the number of speed bumps in crash-prone areas to lower speeds and improve the environment for pedestrians and cyclists. On the main Accra–Kumasi highway, the number of accidents decreased by around 35 per cent, fatalities fell by 55 per cent and serious injuries by 76 per cent, between January 2000 and April 2001 (Afukaar et al 2003; WHO 2009). Reducing the need for motorized travel through sustainable public transport and urban development can be critical in increasing road safety. There is a strong correlation between traffic deaths and the number of kilometres travelled in a vehicle. Compact and accessible buildings and environments, walking and cycling facilities, and good quality public transportation systems reduce the need for motorized travel, and have a positive effect on road safety. The organization of traffic through bus rapid transit (BRT) has shown reductions in injuries and fatalities in places like Bogota and Guadalajara (Duduta, Hidalgo & Adriazola, in press).

Changing drivers' risky behaviours. In 2003, Mexico City's Department of Public Safety in collaboration with the Department of Health Forensics launched *Conduce Sin Alcohol* (Drive without alcohol). This programme was a component of a comprehensive policy to reduce road injuries in the city that followed WHO recommendations on road safety. *Conduce Sin Alcohol* focuses on road interventions often implemented by justice, law enforcement and health authorities that randomly measure alcohol levels among drivers. It is estimated that the programme resulted in a 50 per cent reduction in road fatalities related to alcohol and drugs. To date road injuries have steadily decreased by 20 per cent each year (Valencia et al., 2009). Health authorities contribute to *Conduce Sin Alcohol* undertaking epidemiological surveillance, contributing to the design of awareness campaigns, and providing data to support the work of the public safety authorities to determine areas of increased road incidents (Valencia et al., 2009).

Recommended reading

1. WHO (2009). *Global status report on road safety. Time for action.* Geneva, World Health Organization.
2. WHO (2004). *World report on road traffic injury prevention (2004).* Geneva, World Health Organization.

Useful links

UN Road Safety Collaboration web site launched by the UN General Assembly. WHO acts as its coordinator. The web site includes tools, publications and information on projects, and resources on the recently launched Decade of Action for Road Safety (2011–2020): http://www.who.int/roadsafety/en/

European Commission Road Safety. Web site with resources on different road users, road safety topics, tools and technical information on rod safety: http://ec.europa.eu/transport/road_safety/index_en.htm

Pedestrian and Bicycle Information Center (PBIC). Clearinghouse for information on mobility for pedestrians (including transit users) and cyclists, health and safety, engineering, advocacy, education, enforcement and access. The PBIC is funded by the US Department of Transportation and serves anyone interested in pedestrian and bicycle issues, including planners, engineers, citizens, lawyers, educators, police enforcement and the health community: http://www.walkinginfo.org/

GOAL 3. SUSTAINABLE TRANSPORT SYSTEMS ENSURE EVERYONE CAN ACCESS TRANSPORT SERVICES AND FACILITIES WITHOUT BARRIERS

TRANSPORT SYSTEMS SHOULD BE DESIGNED TO SERVE THE NEEDS OF ALL PEOPLE, ADDRESSING THE BARRIERS THAT PREVENT MOBILITY, ESPECIALLY FOR DISADVANTAGED GROUPS.

Transport challenges and responses

Transport accessibility refers to the differences in people's ability to reach goods, services and destinations (Litman, 2011). Often, the built-in conditions of transport systems impact on people's capacity to access to them. At a macro level, unplanned urban growth or the focus exclusively on a specific transport option (e.g. private vehicles) can leave large population groups with no transport. Thus, policy-makers are faced with the challenge of addressing the needs of different population groups and making transport accessible for all.

Large scale, unplanned urbanization often leaves large urban areas poorly serviced by transport and with poor quality roads. Evidence shows that accessibility is unequally distributed across all societies. Overall, richer countries have higher rates of motorization and thus higher rates of accessibility. Yet, about 30 per cent of the population of affluent countries, such as the United Kingdom and the United States, does not have access to their own car (Banister, 2009). Precise measures of ownership in low- and middle-income countries were not found, but it is very likely that this number is higher than in high-income countries. This impedes the ability of poor and disadvantaged groups in all countries regardless of their income level to access employment opportunities, as well as much needed health and social services. It also increases the cost of their mobility in terms of commuting hours and fares.

Health status or conditions can also act as a direct barrier to access. Transport systems that do not take into consideration the needs of people with limited mobility (due to health status, disabilities, age or any other consideration) are less used by these groups. While international and national legislative frameworks mandate governments to adopt measures to enable the mobility of people with disabilities, implementation in lower income countries is poor. These issues become more of a concern given current global population ageing trends. In general, the promotion of better accessibility requires the following interventions.

(i) The identification of the nature of access barriers operating at the societal level (e.g. cost, distance, conditions, timing, etc.) and appropriate interventions. Common measures to improve access include investments in public transport, the promotion of non-motorized transport or regulatory measures and incentives. For example, fee waivers encourage mobility of the elderly and other vulnerable groups in Geneva, Switzerland, where free public transport is provided to those who accompany an elderly person (WHO, 2007a). The design and expansion of transport systems can be better implemented in the context of urban planning phases to ensure that the upgrading or development of transport options takes into account the needs and demands of all social groups. A design criteria frequently used is whether the proposed transport option allows all people to reach destinations, and economic and social activities in less time (e.g. 'smart growth') (Litman, 2011).

(ii) At the level of the individual, the design of physical elements adapted to the different needs of people with limited mobility. This includes mandatory design standards or codes that transport systems must adopt to enable those with reduced mobility to take full advantage of as many transport opportunities as possible. The adoption of the concept of 'Universal Design' can integrate the needs of people with limited mobility (Frye, 2011). This concept advocates that the design of products and environments be usable by all people to the greatest extent possible, without the need for adaptation (Mace, 1998). Universal design was first introduced for housing codes and expanded to other areas including transport systems. It is based on the principles of equitable use, flexibility in use, simple and intuitive features, perceptible information, tolerance for error, low physical effort and adequate size and space for approach and use (Mace, 1998). For example, low floor buses, colour contrast on stanchions and step edges and non-slip surfaces are some features of universal design applied to transport that can facilitate the use of public transport by people with disabilities, elderly people and parents with children (Frye, 2011).

Policy-makers often monitor impacts by exploring transport patterns of population groups stratified by age, sex, income, location, disability or impairments. For example, Mishra (2011) studied the transport needs of women and men by income and trip patterns in different Indian cities. She found that male commuters used transport mainly for work-related needs, while women, in addition to work-related needs, used transport for errands and to assist dependants (e.g. to gain access to groceries, schools, child care, health services). While men and women travel at 'peak hours', women also travel at off-peak hours but, as might be expected, transport supply at off-peak hours was lower (Mishra, 2011; Peters, 1998).

Examples of health impacts and pathways

Affordability of transport impacting on disposable income for food and medical care. A study in the United States on the housing and transportation costs of working-class families in 28 metropolitan areas found that on average families spent 29 per cent of their incomes on transport. They only spent 15.1 per cent on food and 7.7 per cent on health care. The study covered 47.1 million households and concluded that excessive transport costs often related to people's preference for private cars, limited their consumption of healthy foods and their ability to seek appropriate medical care (Lipman, 2006).

Facilitating mobility for access to health services. The availability of transport plays a key role in accessing health care, and in achieving health targets in the MDGs. Studies on maternal health (MDG 5) acknowledge the role that poor transport networks plays in maternal mortality (Coleman et al., 2011; Ikegami, 2003; ICDDR,B, 2005). For example, in Indonesia, in two villages in Banten Province (204 women), 64 per cent of women living near a paved road received antenatal care services from a trained midwife, compared to 38 percent of those who lived close to a non-paved road that did not have access to such services (Babinard & Roberts, 2006; Ishimori, 2003).

Reduced transport accessibility, physical activity and health. Lack of conveniently accessible transport limits leisure time and time for physical activity, which are both important for good health. A study in Perth, Australia, of 1803 adults aged 18-59, assessed the frequency and duration of vigorous and light-to-moderate activity and walking for recreation. It was found that these activities were inversely related to the distance and attractiveness of open public spaces, green areas, location, as well as access to transport (Giles-Corti, 2005). Studies from Gambia, Brazil, Ghana, Nigeria and Sierra Leone show that poor transport contributes to perinatal mortality (Cham, Sundby & Vangen, 2005). The timing of medical interventions in obstetric emergencies is crucial in avoiding death and disability. In these countries, both health and transport practitioners have planned how to deploy roads to connect health facilities with populations to reduce fatalities (Cham, Sundby & Vangen, 2005). Although these are not institutionalized collaborative initiatives, they prove that coordination can contribute to improving health and transport goals.

Barriers preventing transport usage by elderly people. Loss of personal independent mobility among elderly people is associated with increased mental and physical decline and depression (Kaiser, 2009). Increasing connectivity is especially important for ageing societies. Measures that support elderly people's travel can also reduce health-care costs (WHO, 2002).

In San José, Costa Rica, health researchers found that the lack of shelters at transport stops was an important barrier to older people using public transport. In Shanghai, the People's Republic of China, the lack of seating areas at bus stops was identified as an important barrier to elderly people accessing the public transport system and leading active lives (WHO, 2002; 2007a). Pavements, pedestrian ways and bus shelters are also elements that affect older people's access to transport. This was highlighted in a study of 33 cities carried out by WHO (2007a; 2007b) that found an association between pavement conditions and the number of falls.

Transport barriers impeding disabled people's access to health services. A study in Uttar Pradesh and Tamil Nadu, India, found that the cost of health care (70.5 per cent), lack of health services in the area (52.3 per cent), and transportation (20.5 per cent) were the top three barriers to using health services for people with disabilities (WHO, 2011a). Studies in southern Africa identified lack of transport as one of the reasons for people with physical disabilities not using health services (WHO, 2011a).

Box 3. SOCIAL DETERMINANTS AND EQUITY FOCUS

Transport costs can be a major share of total costs of health care. An eight-month study of the cost of tuberculosis treatment (DOTS) for households in urban areas in the United Republic of Tanzania found that transport fares were a key barrier to accessing different aspects of the treatment regime (Figure 3). This represented almost 30 per cent of the total out-of-pocket costs directly associated with the treatment (Wyss et al., 2001).

Figure 3. Cost of DOTS treatment for tuberculosis in the United Republic of Tanzania

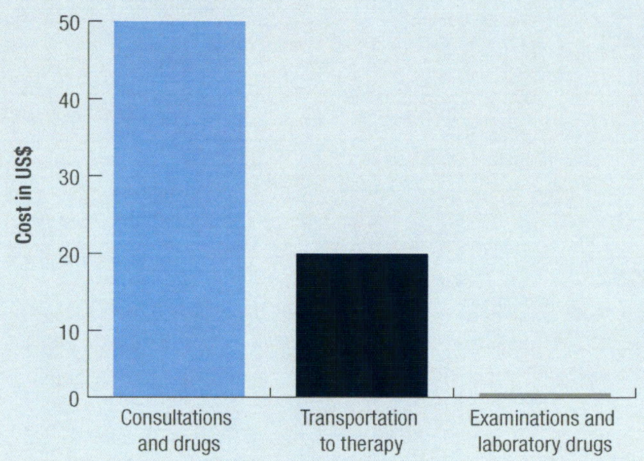

Source: PAHO (2009).

What can both sectors do together?

Design active transport for improved access and health. The availability of walking and cycling choices and the promotion of safe road users' behaviours can improve both equity in access to transport systems and health outcomes. The well designed footpaths and cycling lanes in countries such as Colombia, Sweden and the Netherlands are good examples of this (Lindström, 2008). Both health and transport experts can promote the design of better environments for non-motorized transport users, who, as mentioned earlier, are disadvantaged by current transport trends in terms of transport accessibility.

Provide information on health impacts resulting from improved access to public transport. Lagos, Nigeria (population 15 million), has 2600 kilometres of roads that are congested by a million vehicles daily. The lack of a formal public transport system was affecting the working and living conditions of the population. Growth of the private vehicle fleet, informal transport services and motorcycles had resulted in a chaotic and expensive transport system. The introduction of a BRT scheme in 2008 achieved unprecedented success (200 000 daily passengers). The first phase in service is a 22-kilometre corridor segregated from the other traffic. The system allowed significant improvement in mobility, congestion was greatly reduced, as 35 per cent fewer buses were needed, fares dropped by 30 per cent, travel time was reduced by 35 per cent and waiting time at stops fell by 55 per cent during off-peak hours, and by 73 per cent during peak hours (Trans-Africa Consortium, 2010). These types of interventions provide opportunities for the health experts to assist transport authorities in assessing their health impacts.

Working together to address transport barriers to health care. A recent review of social determinants that impact on the effectiveness of different public health programmes has shown that transport costs are an important financial barrier that often prevent access to health-care services among the poor (Blas & Sivasankara Kurup, 2010). For example, most of the costs of tuberculosis (TB) treatment are incurred before patients reach a health facility. Although in many low- and middle-income countries TB treatment is highly subsidized, subsidies commonly include direct costs for medical tests, medicines, and consultation fees (Lönnroth et al., 2010). Transport costs are not always included. This oversight is also reported for a diversity of public health programmes including alcohol reduction programmes (Schmidt et al., 2010), cardiovascular diseases prevention and treatment (Mendis & Banerjee, 2010), maternal and child health services (Barros et al., 2010) and mental health programmes (Patel et al., 2010). The health sector can help to rectify it by approaching authorities in the transport and social services sectors to advocate for or design initiatives to subsidize the cost of transportation and remove a barrier to people's access to health-care services (e.g. transport vouchers, transport costs reimbursements, etc).

Transport and health authorities conduct joint Health Impact Assessments (HIA) for deprived communities. A Health Impact Assessment, commissioned by transport and health authorities, of a planned transport policy in Edinburgh, the United Kingdom, found that moderate budget increases to implement fee waivers or supplement services could promote more accessible transport for deprived families. It also found that elderly people from low-income groups could increase their physical activity and become less isolated (Gorman et al., 2003). The assessment resulted in a joint decision by transport and health authorities on a budget to promote the implementation of measures to improve accessibility for marginalized groups.

Hold training workshops to improve independent travel in elderly populations. The identification of the nature of barriers to the elderly's independent travel and the design of interventions requires the active assistance of health. In 2010, a series of measures were introduced in Kraków, Poland, to facilitate elderly people's use of the public transport system. At rush hours, they placed travel assistants in stations and on public transport to provide information, assist at vending machines and serve as guides. The public health authorities organized training seminars on vulnerable road users and on the promotion of elderly people's mobility.

Fieldwork on new transport tools to audit accessibility. In New Zealand, the transport agency developed tools for auditing public transport accessibility. As a result of intersectoral collaboration during the field work that was undertaken to develop these tools, health and safety issues were included as part of the auditing tools. Access to health-care services is one of the indicators measured (O'Fallon, 2010). More generally, input from health professionals improved transport policy-makers' understanding of the areas of health and well-being to explore for monitoring purposes.

Recommended reading

1. Canadian Human Rights Commission (2006). *International best practices in universal design: a global review.* Ottawa, ON.
2. WHO (2011). *World report on disability.* Geneva, World Health Organization.
3. WHO-EURO (2006). *Collaboration between the health and transport sectors in promoting physical activity: examples from European countries.* Copenhagen, WHO Regional Office for Europe.

Useful links

WHO-EURO web site on physical activity with information, research findings, resources on physical activity and active transport: http://www.euro.who.int/en/what-we-do/health-topics/disease-prevention/physical-activity

EuroAccess is a project funded by the European Union to advance the accessibility of public transport for people with disabilities. Useful information and resources including a review of policies and regulations, information on user needs, best practices and cost benefit analyses: http://www.euro-access.org/index.html

Access Exchange International (AEI). NGO that supports accessible transport for people with limited mobility. The web site has a resources section with technical publications for practitioners and 130 links on design and accessible transport: http://www.globalride-sf.org/index.html

GOAL 4. TRANSPORT SYSTEMS PROMOTE ENVIRONMENTALLY SUSTAINABLE TRANSPORT OPTIONS

TRANSPORT SHOULD ENSURE MOBILITY BY ADOPTING ENVIRONMENTALLY SOUND SYSTEMS AND MODES.

Transport challenges and responses

Increasing carbon emissions from transport are affecting the global climate with irreversible health consequences (Banister & Woodcock, 2011). Transport policy-makers are challenged with the need to reduce and eliminate these affects on the environment and health, while expanding transport networks. This makes the case to use less carbon in our energy consumption (Banister, 2005). This implies expanding public transport systems, and supporting cycling and walking, especially for urban populations.

Main pollutants are: (i) nitrogen oxides (linked to respiratory problems and reduced lung function); (ii) volatile organic compounds (VOCs) such as methane and ethylene (linked to reduced respiratory function, irritation and photochemical smog); (iii) carbon monoxide (linked to difficulties in oxygen absorption and fertility problems); (iv) particulate matter or PM (particles coming mainly from diesel fuels, tyre particles and road dust that are less than 10 millionths of a metre -µm- across and small enough to get into the lungs (PM10), and are linked to premature mortality, respiratory and cardiovascular diseases, and asthma); and (v) other pollutants like lead (Pb), ammonia (NH3), and sulphur dioxide (SO2), which are being reduced by using 'cleaner' engines, but are still linked to low mental development in children and to bronchitis (Dora & Phillips, 2000; Hosking et al, 2011; Banister & Woodcock, 2011; WHO-EURO, 2006).

In addition to pollutants and CO2 emissions, transport policy-makers are confronted with the burden of disease from noise pollution, which is linked to cardiovascular diseases (PAHO, 2009). Noise and vibration also affect social interaction, economic activities and the integrity of buildings. As already mentioned, road enlargement also impacts on land use restricting people's movement, and undermining community life and land use (Hunter, Farrington & Walton, 2001).

A key intervention is the reduction of the overall use of motorized vehicles and specifically private vehicles. Measures like the adoption of cleaner fuels will mitigate some of the impacts but they will be outweighed by increases in the volume of motorized transport. Measures to reduce the use of motorized vehicles include the introduction of environmentally friendly public transport systems, the promotion of cycling and walking, and economic disincentives such as smaller car parking facilities and higher charges for parking. Interventions aimed at minimizing private motor vehicle energy consumption per capita include reducing travel distances, improving engines and encouraging car sharing. Policy-makers can also adopt legislation that restricts the source of pollutants by regulating emission rates for vehicles of different ages. Better roads design and land use designation also has an impact on pollution, including noise. Other measures to address noise include traffic calming and the construction of sound barriers.

Examples of health impacts and pathways

Air quality and mortality. Global burden of disease (GBD) estimates indicate that air pollution from non-domestic sources accounts for 1.4 per cent of global mortality (Ostro, 2004; WHO, 2011a; WHO-EURO, 2006). A study in Thailand using data related to six million deaths over a period of eight years showed that 29 per cent of cardiovascular disease deaths could be linked to non-domestic air pollution (WHO, 2008). Another study in the United States estimated that 22 million people suffering from asthma yearly resulted in about 14 million days of missed school. Asthma is more common among children, women and girls, African Americans, and those living below the poverty level. Health costs related to poor air quality due to emissions from transport are on average US$ 52 billion per year for the country (APHA, 2010).

Socioeconomic position, place of residence and pollution. Transport-related pollution, place of residence and mortality are often linked (APHA, 2010; Pope et al., 2002). People living close to airports, highways and busy roads more often belong to low-socioeconomic groups. Research shows that they are more likely to be exposed to pollution and to develop respiratory conditions. Also, they face more adverse environmental conditions, such as land degradation and deforestation (Tiwari 2002; WHO 2008; Wong CM et al., 2008). The same groups are more likely to lack access to suitable transport, take longer to commute to work, which is linked to stress and physical ailments, such as back pain and heart disease (APHA, 2010).

Noise and health. In relation to noise, cumulative exposure, even at low levels, is annoying and disturbs sleep (PAHO, 2009). At a higher intensity, noise leads to mental health disorders and physical effects such as increased blood pressure (WHO-EURO, EC, 2011).

What can both sectors do together?

Contribute to the regulation of mandatory vehicle standards. The health sector can contribute to the work of transport authorities in adopting and implementing standards for environment protection. The California Air Resources Board (ARB) passed regulations in 2010 that required trucks to reduce smog-producing emissions of soot and nitrous oxides. The regulations required large trucks to be equipped with aerodynamic technologies such as low-rolling resistance tyres, skirts and fairings. Tractors and trailers with aerodynamic technologies are more fuel efficient, and are estimated to save about three billion gallons of diesel fuel nationwide. From 2010 to 2020, it is expected that this will reduce 33 million metric tons of CO2 emissions. Health practitioners have contributed to the development of this regulation with evidence on the health consequences of air pollution, and take part in the decision-making processes of the California Air Resources Board.

Box 4. SOCIAL DETERMINANTS AND EQUITY FOCUS

In many urban areas in low- and middle-income countries, transport systems are identified as one of the most important sources of environmental pollutants. They are linked to asthma, chronic obstructive pulmonary disease, lung cancer, atherosclerosis, ischemic heart disease and stroke (Garg, 2011). Prevalence and exposure to these risks are unequally distributed among population groups. Figure 4 shows the social gradient in respiratory-related deaths in Delhi, India, by income group*.

Figure 4. Deaths and attributed causes per 1000 persons for urban areas in Delhi, India, 1999

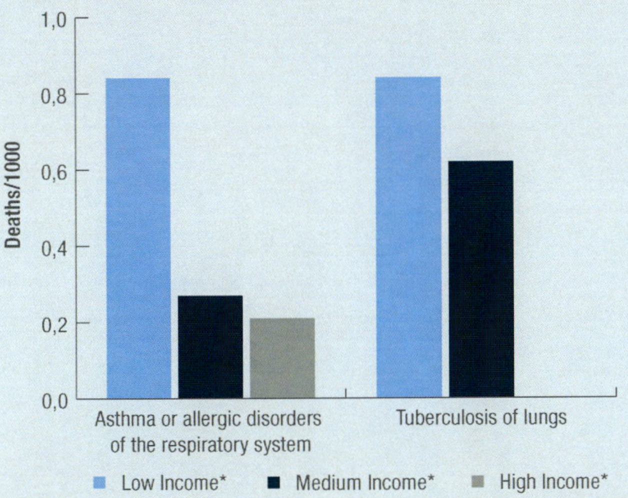

*As defined by the World Bank: LOW (people living on less than US$ 1 purchasing power parity (PPP)/capita/day income); MEDIUM (between US$ 1 and 2 PPP/capita/day income); and HIGH (above US$ 2 PPP/capita/day income) in India for 1999–2000 for a consistency check.

Source: Garg (2011).

Contribute to regulations for and enforcement of air quality standards. Regulations pertaining to the quality of engines and emissions standards are often coupled with measures to eliminate certain pollutants. In Mexico, the National Emissions Inventory (an intersectoral initiative to jointly implement activities aimed at improving air quality and health) monitors the implementation of legal reforms such as the banning of leaded gasoline, the reduction of gasoline sulphurs, and the introduction of natural gas to reduce air pollution. In this area, health authorities can contribute data and skills to measure the public health impacts of such regulations. The health sector participated in the planning and implementation of measures, for example, the phasing out of the leaded gasoline in Mexico and the reduction of sulphurs in diesel (Fernández-Bremauntz, 2005).

Supporting conversion to cleaner fuels Emissions from transport are a critical environmental problem in many cities. The city of Medellin, Colombia, and its surrounding nine municipalities, for example, had high air pollution levels that exceeded legal maximum levels. It was estimated that 65 per cent of the total pollutants in the city were linked to transportation. Impacts on health included nose, throat and eyes irritation, upper respiratory infections, such as bronchitis and pneumonia, as well as allergic reactions. People with asthma or emphysema were at most risk of aggravating their medical conditions. In 2001, the city government and the public utility company launched a subsidies programme for vehicle owners to shift to cleaner fuels (natural gas). By 2007, more than 22 000 vehicles (15 per cent of the fleet) had been converted to natural gas (Saldarriaga & Vergara, 2008). Similar policies have been in place in Peru since 2005, and in Argentina and Brazil for at least three decades. Conversion to cleaner fuels and technologies cannot alone reduce the environmental impacts of transport as increasing motorization can offset progress made by cleaner fuels (Banister, 2005). Yet, in the context of comprehensive transport policies that promote non-motorized transport and public transport systems that consider the needs of pedestrians, the health sector can work together with transport authorities when designing programmes for conversion to cleaner fuels. The health sector can provide evidence on the positive or negative health impacts of the different policy options being considered and monitor progress.

Noise reduction via more public transport. Studies show that most noise pollution comes from private motor vehicles. A common measure to decrease noise is the introduction or expansion of public transport systems (PAHO, 2009). From 2000 to 2008, in Bogotá, Colombia, bus rapid transport systems lowered the city's overall noise pollution by approximately 30 per cent (BRTPC, 2009). Health and transport sectors can work together to monitor noise standards and design sound public health/transport interventions.

Support the adoption of active transport policies. Private vehicles contribute the largest share of carbon emissions in the transport sector. Data suggest that active transport would have a greater impact on reducing emissions than increasing the use of low-emission cars (Woodcock et al., 2009). The promotion of emission-free active transport such as walking or cycling, is a strategy that health, environment and transport authorities can jointly explore. The campaign 'Walking and Cycling' launched by the Department of Transport, the United Kingdom, estimated that a reduction of eight driven kilometres reduces 1.5 per cent of all transport-related emissions. Health authorities can support transport authorities in assessing the role of physical activity, safe walking and cycling in urban areas to advance sustainable transport policies. As mentioned in Goal 1, health authorities can provide guidelines and tools to help transport authorities quantify the health effects of cycling and walking or calculate the economic impacts of cycling to complement existing economic evaluation tools. Austria, the Czech Republic, New Zealand, Sweden, the United Kingdom and the United States, for example, have adopted similar tools to improve the sustainability of transport systems (WHO-EURO, 2007).

Recommended reading

1. Hosking J et al. (2011). Health in the green economy, health co-benefits of climate change mitigation - transport sector. Geneva, World Health Organization.
2. Dora C, Phillips M, eds. (2000). Transport, environment and health. Copenhagen, WHO Regional Office for Europe.
3. UNEP (2011). *Towards a green economy: pathways to sustainable development and poverty eradication.* Geneva, United Nations Environment Programme.

Useful links

US Environmental Protection Agency. Office of Transport and Air Quality (OTAQ) reconciles the transportation sector with the environment, advancing clean fuels and technology, and working to promote more livable communities: http://www.epa.gov/oms/

International Transport Forum (ITF). Inter-governmental organization within the OECD. A global think tank for transport issues that brings together 52 countries to advance a sustainable global transport policy agenda. It facilitates the exchange of information among transport stakeholders undertaking economic research, data collection, statistical studies and policy analysis, often in collaboration with academia, business and government entities: http://www.internationaltransportforum.org/home.html

GOAL 5. SUSTAINABLE TRANSPORT SYSTEMS PROMOTE MOBILITY CONDUCIVE TO LIVELIHOOD SECURITY AND LIVEABLE COMMUNITIES

TRANSPORT SYSTEMS SHOULD CONTRIBUTE TO SOCIAL COHESION BY ADDRESSING CONGESTION; IMPROVING PUBLIC TRANSPORT SYSTEMS AND POLICIES AIMED AT REDUCING CAR USE; DEVELOPING INFRASTRUCTURE FOR PEDESTRIANS AND CYCLISTS; AND BY ENCOURAGING SOCIAL INTERACTION AND LIVELIHOOD SECURITY.

Transport challenges and responses

Mobility is fundamental to communities and to people's quality of life. It allows them to socialize and access jobs, markets, schools, and open spaces, such as parks or other natural environments. In addressing liveability, transport policy-makers face the challenge of balancing motorized and non-motorized transport users' needs, and of ensuring that it applies to all communities. The challenge is large. Social interactions are vital for health and well-being (Holt-Lunstad et al., 2010). In many countries, the increase in motorization combined with urban sprawl has resulted in levels of congestion and 'community severance' that has diminished the liveability of communities.

Several interventions mentioned in Goals 3 and 4 are needed to address this goal. For instance, to address congestion, interventions related to motor vehicles include priority user policies (e.g. special bus lanes or specific vehicles in specific roads) or pricing policies (e.g. road pricing and parking controls). Of these, the latter have been found to be the most effective way to reduce congestion in specific local communities (Saleh, 2007). Controls on parking spaces aimed at reducing congestion are implemented by city authorities and limit the number of spaces, the duration of parking, the cost of parking and priority users. However, to be effective these controls need constant monitoring and enforcement.

Other interventions that promote active transport and mobility involve Transit-Oriented Developments (TODs) also called Transport Development Areas (TDAs), that promotes densification alongside mixed land uses. TODs promote the use of public transport and encourage high-density and compact cities where walking and non-motorised transport is complemented with public transport. TODs are linked to housing and economic policies and try to confront the problems created by urban sprawl through the creation of communities with multiple zoning where people live, work and have a social life, promoting social interaction and less car dependence (Lund et al., 2004).

Another group of relevant interventions are BRT schemes that set up networks of high speed buses on segregated rights of way that allow people to move faster than in private motor vehicles. These schemes require enhancements in infrastructure, transport scheduling and information for users, and often use dedicated bus lanes to improve mobility and decrease congestion.

Finally, enhancing people's ability to walk and cycle is a key aspect of active transport interventions. As mentioned previously, this means increasing the extent and quality of the space used by the public to travel by foot, bicycle or other non-motorized transport. In general, they encourage the increased availability of green or open spaces as well as safe direct, continuous and attractive routes. Integration among the different modes of transport, especially non-motorized transport with high quality mass transit is key to improving current conditions and attracting more users. An example of this would be well designed and guarded bicycle parking facilities in mass transit stations. All of these interventions require policy-makers to develop appropriate legal frameworks to sustain the interventions (PAHO, 2009).

Examples of health impacts and pathways

The restructuring of spaces and reduced social interactions. Social interactions are vital for health and well-being (Holt-Lunstad et al., 2010). These interactions very often also take place in the public space such as streets, pavements or parks. Transport systems that bisect communities and reduce public areas can restructure community space reducing social interactions, and increasing psychosocial stress. In his landmark study 'Livable Streets' in San Francisco, the United States, Appleyard (1981) demonstrated that individuals living in light traffic streets (up to 2000 cars/day) had more friends and acquaintances than people living in medium (up to 8000 cars/day) and heavy traffic (up to 16 000 cars/day) streets.

Urban sprawl and reduced space for physical activity. A study in the United States comprising 206 000 adults (448 counties in 83 metropolitan areas) found that residents of sprawling counties walked less, weighed more and had higher prevalence of hypertension than residents of compact cities (Ewing et al., 2006). Less physical activity, results in higher rates of obesity, which in turn is linked to greater car usage and thus to more emissions (Frank, Kavage & Litman, 2006; Woodcock et al., 2009). Urban design is a key factor in encouraging physical activity (Heath et al., 2006).

Communities with active commuting opportunities and reduced cardiovascular diseases. A recent systematic review found that active commuting (walking or cycling) had a robust protective effect on cardiovascular outcomes (Hammer & Chida 2008) in populations of high-income countries. However, evidence suggests that most active commuters are of higher educational levels (Gordon-Larsen et al., 2009). Expanding active transport reduces congestion within communities, promoting interaction and physical activity, and ensuring people's access to livelihoods (PAHO, 2009; Khayesi, Monheim & Nebe, 2010). For example a recent analysis estimated that almost 1.8 million jobs were accessed on foot within 20 minutes from a major public transport station in New York, nearly 400 000 in London and almost 200 000 in Beijing (Mehndiratta & Darido, 2011).

Transit-Oriented Developments, Bus Rapid Transits and reduced mortality. Curitiba, Brazil, started to implement TOD schemes in 1965 and in the mid-1970s adopted one of the first BRT systems in the world. By 2010, the BRT was accommodating 70 per cent of Curitiba's commuters (PAHO, 2009). In 15 years, pedestrian fatalities per 10 000 vehicles had decreased from 427 in 1970 to 93 in 1985 (Gold, 1999). Moreover, this indicator was 4.1 in 2002 (Souza & Carvalho de Lima, 2006). In the case of Bogota, Colombia, the introduction of the BRT system, along with other sustainable transport measures such as extensive facilities for walking and cycling, car restrictions and fuel price increases were critical in reducing fatalities from 914 in 1998 to 486 in 2007 (PAHO, 2010).

Road pricing and healthier active transport. Road pricing was introduced in London, the United Kingdom, in 2003. As of 2009, traffic entering the charging zone had been reduced by 21 per cent, cycling had increased by 43 per cent and public transport had accommodated the displaced car users (Nurul, 2009). Lower emission levels and increases in physical exercise in the London population have been documented as having positive impacts on health determinants.

Box 5. SOCIAL DETERMINANTS AND EQUITY FOCUS

Low-income populations live in communities that are frequently far from their places of work and have limited access to transport. For example, 70 per cent of people living in communities in the city of Addis Ababa, Ethiopia, and in Lusaka, Zambia, commute on foot (Behrens et al., 2004). A recent study comparing communities of different income levels in cities of Burkina Faso (Ouagadougou), Mali (Bamako), Niger (Niamey), Senegal (Dakar) and South Africa (Cape Town) found that motor-oriented transport policies mostly benefit high-income groups who have access to private vehicles or can afford public transport. Figure 5 shows the distribution of trips by type of mobility and by household income for different areas in Cape Town.

Figure 5. Distribution of modalities of transport by household income, Cape Town, South Africa (percentages)

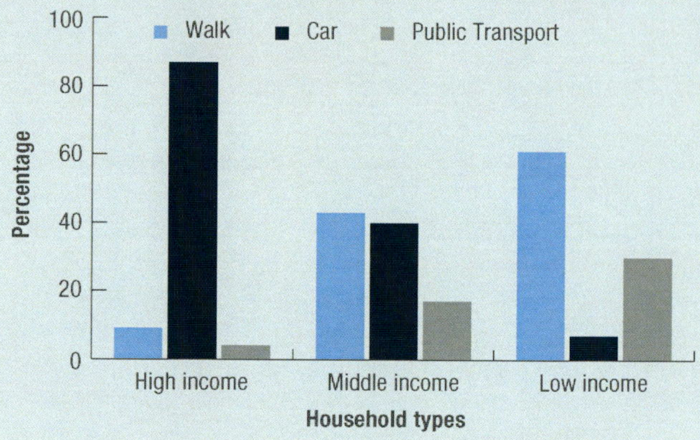

Source: Behrens et al. (2004).

What can both sectors do together?

Participate in the process of land use reforms to benefit non-motorized users. Between 1995 and 2001, the city of Bogota, Colombia, implemented a land use reform process coupled with transport measures and health promotion interventions targeting non-motorized road users and improving public transport. The city built cycling and pedestrian routes and car-free routes. It also created exclusion zones for motor vehicles at peak times and developed a high-capacity bus system. Annual road traffic fatalities decreased by 50 per cent, from 1384 cases to 694 (WHO, 2009). Land use reform processes provide opportunities for both sectors to make changes to mobility patterns that enhance safety and increase community interaction, while decreasing mortality.

Provide health information on impacts of restructured community space to inform policies. In Quito, Ecuador (population 1.4 million), urban sprawl led to an increase in private motor vehicle usage and the introduction of unauthorized vehicles for public transport, which impacted on air quality. Since 1994, the Metrobús-Q system transports 440 000 passengers daily with buses running on exclusive lanes, making public transport faster (PAHO, 2009). Transport systems enable people to access public services such as hospitals or care centres. When expanding a public transport network, both the health and transport sectors need to identify the potential benefits of choosing one or other location. In addition, the health sector can support transport authorities in predicting the health impacts of future transport projects or evaluating existing ones.

Advocacy for cycling and walking spaces. In 1999, the city of Marikina (population 500 000), close to Manila (the Philippines), created the 52 kilometre Marikina Bikeway System (MBS) to reduce congestion and emissions. The system connects residential communities with schools, employment centres, the new metropolitan train station, and other public transport terminals (Karekezi, Majoro & Johnson, 2003). Around 50 000 people use bicycles on a daily basis in the city (World Bank, 2011). This initiative is coupled with the Metro Manila Urban Transport Integration Project that has reduced traffic congestion and travel times. Both the health and transport sectors can take opportunities such as the MBS to promote active transport interventions that reduce congestion and pollution, and increase low-income groups' access to livelihoods. The health sector and WHO have been advocating for increased active transport and have presented the evidence on the impact of greater social connectivity on community health to support this policy choice.

Work with communities to protect and improve liveability in the face of new transport developments. Approximately 20 per cent of the population of Bangkok, Thailand, lives in slums (1.6 million). In 2000, a plan to build a new highway to reduce traffic congestion considered the evictions of a large number of informal settlements along the Bangbua canal. Faced with the destruction of their communities, the residents worked with local authorities, and housing, transport and health ministries to launch a slum upgrading process comprising new housing units, improved sanitation and water facilities, and access to transport infrastructure. The aim of the initiative was to ensure that rather than displacing the communities, the projected highway could be planned in a way that would enhance liveability (WHO, 2008).

Support community organizations to improve liveability. In several sub-Saharan African countries (e.g. Burkina Faso, Ghana, Kenya, Rwanda, Togo and Uganda), civil society organizations have joined forces to promote cycling as a way of addressing the various effects of urban sprawl, including the isolation of individuals within communities. As a result of these actions, Kenya launched the Bicycle Workshop, Cycle to School and Curriculum Development for Bicycle Mechanics projects and Uganda launched the Cycle to School and Bicycle Ambulances projects. These initiatives positively impacted on income generating activities and access to social services (e.g. school and health services). This is an opportunity for health and transport to work together in assessing the external costs of these initiatives and identifying the means to scale them up.

Partner with networks advocating for liveable communities to disseminate and share information. Advocacy is a key action to motivate and keep political commitment to intersectoral work between health and transport sectors. The partnership between the Pan American Health Organization (PAHO), and the Centre for Sustainable Transport (EMBARQ) is an example of how health authorities and transport stakeholders can work together to achieve healthy and sustainable transport systems. This partnership will make use of a established global network of transport centres that promote sustainable transport solutions and quality of life in cities in middle- and low-income countries. These centres work with local transport authorities supporting the linkages between health and transport to reduce pollution and create more liveable communities by providing safe and accessible urban public spaces.

Recommended reading

1. PAHO (2009). *Advocating for safe and healthy public transportation.* Washington, DC, Pan American Health Organization.
2. Levinson HS et al. (2003). *Bus Rapid Transit. Volume 1: case studies in Bus Rapid Transit.* Washington, DC, Transit Cooperative Research Program (http://www.trb.org/Main/Public/Blurbs/152921.aspx, accessed 26 September 2011).
3. Institute for Transportation and Development Policy (2010). *Our cities ourselves. Principles for transport in urban life.* New York, A useful advocacy publication: http://www.itdp.org/documents/OCO8principlesBook_FINAL.pdf

Useful links

International Association of Public Transport (UITP). International network made up of public transport authorities and operators, policy-makers, scientific institutes and industry. It is a global advocate of public transport and sustainable mobility: http://www.uitp.org/

World Resources Institute Center for Sustainable Transport (EMBARQ). Global network of transport research and policy centres that fosters government-business-civil society partnerships for finding solutions to the transportation-related problems in cities. Partnerships identify, test, evaluate and implement solutions to local transport problems: http://www.embarq.org

SUMMARY MESSAGES

Health equity is a guiding principle and catalyst that can contribute to sustainable transport systems and development

- Transport is key for the economy and societies' well-being and health – promoting access to jobs and public services. Yet the design of transport systems can fundamentally determine who benefits more. Increasing public transport and non-motorized mobility promotes accessibility for lower income households and the most vulnerable, while also addressing the important transport issue of congestion. Improved urban density measures, land management and zoning regulations, and the location of employment opportunities are also important. Together they contribute to the sustainability of transport systems and inclusive economic development.

- It is important to increase the visibility of the safety and accessibility needs of marginalized groups and vulnerable road users, including those with disabilities. This requires transport policies oriented towards the needs of non-motorized users. Better regulation of roads and vehicles along with scaled-up investment in public transport interventions can reduce the hardships experienced by more marginalized groups in society (e.g. higher accidents and injury rates, unaffordable transport costs, long commuting hours, reduced access to services, and less time for family life).

- Increasingly, negative environmental impacts from transport are affecting the global climate and the quality of life, especially in low-income communities. Environmental policy-makers advocate the reduction of society's reliance on carbon technologies, which requires transport authorities to promote active non-motorized and public transport. Considering equity issues and the environmental impacts of transport will contribute to sustainable transport systems.

- Policy-makers face the challenge of designing transport systems that maintain or enhance connectivity within and between communities. Liveable communities are an important determinant of health. Promoting a more active voice for non-motorized and public transport users in policy and planning processes will be an essential strategy in these efforts.

- Sustainable transport and urban development practices save lives. Compact and mixed-use urban developments save spaces for walking and cycling, good quality public transport reduces individual motorized travel, which in turn reduces the risk of road injuries and harmful emissions, and increases physical activity.

New role for health in working with transport: cross-cutting functions

The health equity imperative and the intersectoral actions described in this document provide specific examples of a new role for public health, which were outlined in the Adelaide Statement on Health in All Policies (WHO and Government of South Australia, 2010). Public health and transport authorities can expect to reap better returns from health and transport policies if they carry out these functions, which call for better intersectoral collaboration, either more systematically or by developing them where they do not exist. Some notable areas for action include the following:

- monitoring trends and outcomes for populations and specific groups using disaggregated data that uncover the impact of equity on transport policies and to advocate transport sustainability and health;

- encouraging needs-based assessment for disadvantaged populations and specific groups in order to better design actions that increase access to transport and improve health outcomes for hard-to-impact segments of the population;

- developing guidelines, standards and recommendations on transport-related risk factors, and disseminating technical guidance in a spirit of shared responsibility for both health and transport actors;

- supporting the participation and empowerment of transport users to improve transport options, and thereby the determinants of health;

- supporting the dissemination of information on the linkages between sustainable transport systems and health equity to key transport and health stakeholders, which can encourage the inclusion of sustainable transport practices in health policies and vice versa;

- clarifying the transport and health sectors' technical vocabulary that may not be mutually understood.

There are many entry points for health stakeholders to work with transport stakeholders

Table 3 shows several practical examples of how health stakeholders can collaborate with transport stakeholders to help them achieve their goals, and improve health outcomes and health equity.

Table 3. Summary of areas for intersectoral collaboration between health and transport sectors

Economic development	• Transport is key for economic development; it allows the movement of people, goods and services, and enhances individuals' access to economic opportunities. However, it has typically been based on unsustainable patterns of private motor vehicle use. Increased motor vehicle usage need not be coupled with economic growth. More efficient transport options can promote economic growth while reducing congestion and promoting health. • To address the negative impacts of congestion on the economy, and to promote more equitable economic growth requires collaborative policy-making processes involving the transport, health and environment sectors using a common policy frameworks. At the local level, land use planning is critical. Joint processes enable relevant stakeholders to select joint priorities, harmonize mandates and open a channel of dialogue that breaks silo cultures.
Safety	• Around 3500 people die everyday on the road – 90 per cent of whom live in low- and middle-income countries. Road fatalities are influenced by the fact that motor vehicles often share roads with light vehicles, bicycles and pedestrians. Investments in road infrastructure that accommodate the needs of different transport users are required, as are laws enforcing vehicle standards and users' behaviours. • Areas of potential collaboration include supporting legislation that enhances safety such as speed limits, driving licence penalty points schemes, the use of safety devices and awareness campaigns. Health can assess the economic and health impacts of reduced injuries and fatalities, help transport and police authorities in promoting safer road behaviours and support efforts to increase public awareness and compliance.
Accessibility	• In general transport systems are oriented towards the more advantaged in societies, and towards private motor vehicle users. Transport and health authorities share common interests in ensuring disadvantaged groups are able to access transport by promoting both public transport and active transport. People already suffering from health conditions are a special group of interest for the health sector. • Health and transport authorities can jointly identify barriers to access (e.g. cost, distance, convenience, etc.). Active participation in urban planning and land use planning can help to ensure disadvantaged groups are able to reach essential health services in less time. Both sectors can assist in the design of transport infrastructure to ensure access for people with reduced mobility. Health can support the monitoring of the different impacts of transport policies on population groups, which can be stratified by age, sex, income, location, disability or impairments.
Environmental sustainability	• Transport is one of the most important contributors to GHG emissions, and air and noise pollution. The environmental impact of transport systems is also affecting people's relationship with land, and changing livelihoods and the structure of different communities, with concomitant health implications. • Evidence on the health consequences of air or noise pollution, and other social impacts of changing environments can contribute to setting transport standards that protect the environment. Health authorities can support transport authorities to assess the impact of regulations related to polluting substances, in particular, on air quality (e.g. banning of leaded gasoline, reduction of sulphurs in gasoline). Health actors can also join environment and transport stakeholders in the surveillance and monitoring of environmental impacts, and take measures to improve standards, compliance and the design of new interventions.
Liveability and livelihoods	• In many countries increased motorization combined with urban sprawl is resulting in congestion and community severance, making transport systems a liability rather than an asset to communities. Interventions aimed at improving liveability have the potential to benefit disadvantaged communities by reducing local congestion, increasing green and public areas, providing opportunities for social interactions, and creating communities where populations have access to livelihoods. • Health can contribute to the design and implementation of Transit-Oriented Developments (TODs), Transport Development Areas (TDAs), Bus Rapid Transit schemes and 'walkability' enhancement to provide space for pedestrians, bicycles or other non-motorized transport, thereby promoting opportunities for community connectivity. Health authorities can compile and share data to aid in the design of interventions and contribute to processes that provide choice and a variety of options. In evaluating the impacts of different policy options. The two sectors can work together to ensure the participation of disadvantaged groups, and to back greater advocacy for equity promoting options favouring social connectivity and associated health benefits.

REFERENCES

Afukaar FK, Antwi P, Ofosu-Amah S (2003). Pattern of road traffic injuries in Ghana: implications for control. *Injury Control and Safety Promotion*, 10: 69–76.

Anand A, Tiwari G (2006). A gendered perspective of the Shelter–Transport–Livelihood Link: the case of poor women in Delhi. *Transport Reviews*, 26:63–80.

APHA (2010). At the intersection of public health and transportation: promoting healthy transportation policy. Washington, DC, American Association of Public Health.

Appleyard D (1981). *Livable streets*. Berkeley, CA, University of California Press.

Asian Development Bank (2009). Intersections – gender, HIV, and infrastructure operations: lessons learned from selected ADB–financed transport projects. Mandaluyong City.

Babinard J, Roberts, P (2006). *Maternal and child mortality development goals: what can the transport sector do?* Washington, DC, World Bank and Transport Sector Board.

Bailey L, Mokhtarian P, Little A (2008). *The broader connection between public transportation, energy conservation and greenhouse gas reduction*. Fairfax, VA, ICF International, Inc. (A report by ICF International to the American Public Transportation Association (APTA).

Banister D (2005). *Unsustainable transport: city transport in the 21st century*. London, Routledge.

Banister D (2007). Cities, urban form and sprawl: a European perspective. In: *Transport, urban form and economic growth*. Paris, Organisation for Economic Co-operation and Development (European Conference of Ministers of Transport).

Banister D (2009). Conclusion: the dilemmas of sustainable transport. In: Kassens E, ed. *Sustainable transportation: an international perspective* Cambridge, MA, MIT Department of Urban Studies and Planning, pp. 121–124 (Projections, 9, MIT Journal of Planning).

Banister D, Woodcock J (2011). *Sustainable urban transport: integrating environmental, health and equity objectives. In: Environmental health and equity: global strategies and innovation. International Conference to be held in Montreal 29–30th April 2011* (Draft paper for conference and book).

Barros F et al. (2010). Health and nutrition of children: equity and social determinants. In: Blas E, Sivasankara Kurup A, eds. *Equity, social determinants and public health programmes*. Geneva, World Health Organization.

Behrens R et al. (2004). *Meta-analysis of travel of the poor in the west and southern African cities*. Tenth World Conference on Transport Research, Istanbul, 4–8 July, 2004.

Bielich, C (2010). *Cómo influye el sistema laboral de las empresas de transporte público en la problemática del tránsito limeño? Un acercamiento a las dinámicas de trabajo de las empresas de transporte a partir de la liberalización del sector en 1991, Reporte final [How does the labour regime of public transport enterprises influence the problem of road transit in Lima. An approach to the labour dynamics of transport enterprises since the liberalization of the sector in 1991, Final report]*. Lima, Consorcio de Investigación Económica y Social, Instituto de Estudios Peruanos.

Blas E, Sivasankara Kurup A (2010). *Equity, social determinants and public health programmes*. Geneva, World Health Organization.

BRTPC (2009). Bus Rapid Transit [online database]. Washington, DC, Bus Rapid Transit Policy Center.

BTRE (2007). *Estimating urban traffic and congestion cost trends for Australian cities*. Canberra, Bureau of Transport and Regional Economics, Department of Transport and Regional Services.

Cham M, Sundby J, Vangen S (2005). Maternal mortality in the rural Gambia: a qualitative study on access to emergency obstetric care. *Reproductive Health*, Issue 2:3.

Chamon M, Mauro P, Okawa Y (2008). Mass car ownership in the emerging market giants. Economic Policy, 23:243–296.

Cho B, Choi J, Yum YT (2000). Air pollution and hospital admissions for respiratory disease in certain areas of Korea. *Journal of Occupational Health*, 42:185–191.

Coleman B et al. (2011). The difference transport makes to child mortality and preventive healthcare efforts: Riders for Health. *Archives of Disease in Child*, 96: 197–199.

D'Amato G (2010). Urban air pollution and climate change as environmental risk factors of respiratory allergy: an update. *Journal of Investigational Allergology and Clinical Immunology*, 20: 95–102.

Diallo BL et al. (2011). *Prévalence du VIH, facteurs associés et tendances chez les camionneurs entre 2001 et 2007 en Guinée [HIV prevalence, associated risk factors and evolution among truck drivers between 2001 and 2007 in Guinea]. Médecine tropicale: revue du Corps de santé colonial*, 71: 142–146.

Dora C, Philips M, eds. (2000). *Transport, environment and health*. Copenhagen, WHO Regional Office for Europe.

DOT (2006). *Strategic plan: new Ideas for a nation on the move. Fiscal years 2006–2011*. Washington, DC, Department of Transportation.

Dubowitz T et al. (2008). Neighborhood socioeconomic status and fruit and vegetable intake among whites, blacks, and Mexican Americans in the United States. *American Journal of Clinical Nutrition*, 87:1883–1891.

Duduta N, Hidalgo D, Adriazola C (in press). *Sustainable transport saves lives*. Washington, DC, EMBARQ Health and Road Safety Program (World Resources Institute Brief, Issue 1: Road Safety).

EC (2006). *Respecting the rules: better road safety enforcement in the European Union. A consultation paper*. Brussels, European Commission.

ERSO (2010). *Traffic safety basic facts 2010. Single vehicle accidents. DaCoTA: Project co-financed by the European Commission, Directorate-General for Mobility & Transport*. Brussels, European Commission Road Safety Observatory.

EuroAccess (2008). Best Practice. Innovation and related cost benefit analysis. Project for a European accessibility of public transport for people with disabilities. Brussels, European Union.

Ewing R et al. (2006). Relationship between urban sprawl and physical activity, obesity, and morbidity. *American Journal of Health Promotion*, 18:47–57.

Fernández-Bremauntz A (2005*). Air quality management in Mexico. International perspectives on air quality: risk management principles for policy development*. Mexico City, DF, National Institute for Ecology Research on Urban, Regional and Global Pollution.

FHWA (2000). Operations story. Washington, DC, US Department of transportation, Federal Highway Administration. Available at http://www.ops.fhwa.dot.gov/aboutus/opstory.htm, accessed 3 October 2011).

Fiedler M, Fenton B (2011). Staying mobile: a guide to mobility management in ageing societies. Szentendre, Hungary, The Regional Environmental Center for Central and Eastern Europe.

Frank L, Kavage S, Litman T (2006). *Promoting public health through smart growth: building healthier communities through transportation and land use policies and practices.* Vancouver, BC, Smart Growth BC.

Frye A (2011). *Mobility: rights obligations and equity in an ageing society.* Paris, International Transport Forum.

Garg A (2011). Pro-equity effects of ancillary benefits of climate change policies: a case study of human health impacts of outdoor air pollution in New Delhi. *World Development*, 39:1002–1025.

Giles-Corti B et al. (2005). Increasing walking: how important is distance to, attractiveness, and size of public open space? *American Journal of Preventive Medicine*, 28:169–176.

Gold PA (1999). *Traffic safety: using engineering to reduce accidents.* Washington, DC, Inter-American Development Bank.

Gordon-Larsen P (2009). Active commuting and cardiovascular disease risk: The CARDIA study. *Archives of Internal Medicine*, 169:1216–1223.

Gorman D et al. (2003). Transport policy and health inequalities: a health impact assessment of Edinburgh's transport policy. *Public Health,* 117:15–24.

GRSP (2010). *Annual Report 2010.* Geneva, Global Road Safety Partnership.

Hammer M, Chida Y (2008). Active commuting and cardiovascular risk: a meta-analytic review. *Preventive Medicine*, 46:9–13.

Heath GW et al. (2006) The effectiveness of urban design and land use and transport policies and practices to increase physical activity: a systematic review. *Journal of Physical Activity and Health*, 3(Suppl. 1):S55–S76.

Holm-Hadulla F (2005). *Why transport matters. Contributions of the transport sector to towards achieving the Millenium Development Goals.* Eschborn, Deutsche Gesellschaft für Technische Zusammenarbeit (GTZ) and Federal Ministry for Economic Cooperation and Development.

Hosking E et al (in press). *Health in the green economy, health co-benefits of climate change mitigation - transport sector.* Geneva, World Health Organization.

Holt-Lunstad J, Smith T, Layton, JB (2010). Social relationships and mortality risk: a meta-analytic review. *PLoS Med*, 7:e1000316.

Hoyle B, Smith J (2001). Transport and development: conceptual frameworks. In: Hoyle B, Knowles R, eds. *Modern transport geography,* 2nd ed. Chichester, United Kingdom, Wiley.

Hunter C, Farrington J, Walton W (2001). Transport and the environment. In: Hoyle B, Knowles R, eds. *Modern transport geography,* 2nd ed. Chichester, United Kingdom, Wiley.

ICF Consulting (2003). *Costs-benefit analysis of road safety improvements. Final Report.* London.

IEA (2009). *Transport, energy and CO2.* Paris, International Energy Agency.

IEA (2010). *Energy technology perspectives 2010. scenarios & strategies to 2050.* Paris, International Energy Agency.

IFAD (2008). *High food prices: impact and recommendations for actions. Paper prepared by FAO, IFAD and WFP for the meeting of the Chief Executives Board for Coordination held in Bern, Switzerland, on 28–29 April 2008.* Rome, International Fund for Agricultural Development.

Ikegami K (2003). *The Impact of road development on the health of pregnant and parturient women. Thematic evaluation.* Tokyo, Japan International Cooperation Agency.

ICDDR-B (2005) International Centre for Diarrhoeal Disease Research, Bangladesh. Posting of trained birthing attendants: a comparison of home- and facility-based obstetric care. *Health and Science Bulletin*, 3:11–16.

IRTAD (2010). *Annual report 2010.* Paris, International Traffic Safety Data and Analysis Group.

Ishimori K. (2003). *The impact of road eevelopment on the health of pregnant and parturient women. Results from collaborative research project between The Japan Bank for International Cooperation (JBIC) and the United Nations Population Fund (UNFPA).* New York, NY, United Nations Population Fund (July–October).

Jabbari H et al. (2010). Lack of HIV infection among truck drivers in Iran using rapid HIV test. *Journal of Medical Sciences Research*, 15:287–289.

Jacobs G, Aeron-Thomas A, Astrop A (2000). *Estimating global road fatalities.* Crowthorne, United Kingdom, Transport Research Laboratory.

Kahlmeier S (2011). "Health in All Policies" in practice: guidance and tools to quantifying the health effects of cycling and walking. *Journal of Physical Activity and Health,* 7(Suppl. 1):S120–S125.

Karekezi S, Majoro L, Johnson T (2003). *Climate change and urban transport: priorities for the World Bank.* Washington, DC, African Energy Policy Research Network & Environment Department, World Bank.

Kenworthy J, Townsend C (2002). An international comparative perspective on motorization in urban China. Problems and Prospects. *ATSS Research*, 26:99–109.

Khayesi M, Monheim H, Nebe JM. (2010). Negotiating „Streets for All" in urban transport planning: the case for pedestrians, cyclists and street vendors in Nairobi, Kenya. *Antipode*, 42:103–126.

Lacerda R et al. (1997). Truck drivers in Brazil: prevalence of HIV and other sexually transmitted diseases, risk behavior and potential for spread of infection. *AIDS*, 11(Suppl. 1):S15–S19.

Lemey P et al. (2003). *Tracing the origin and history of the HIV-2 epidemic. Proceedings of the National Academy of Sciences of the United States of America*, 100:6588–6592.

Lindström M (2007). Means of transportation to work and overweight and obesity: a population-based study in southern Sweden. *Preventive Medicine*, 46:22–28.

Lipman B (2006). *A heavy load: the combined housing and transportation burdens of working families.* Washington, DC, Center for Housing Policy (http://www.nhc.org/pdf/pub_heavy_load_10_06.pdf, accessed 28 September 2011).

Litman T (2011). *Evaluating accessibility for transportation planning. Measuring people's ability to reach desired goods and activities.* Victoria, BC, Victoria Transport Policy Institute.

Liu L (2005). Chapter 7. Towards sustainable urban transport in China: the role of Bus Rapid Transit Systems. In: Jonson G, Tengstrom E , eds. *Urban transport development. A complex issue.* New York, NY, Springer.

Lönnroth et al. (2010). Tuberculosis: the role of risk factors and social determinants. In: Blas E, Sivasankara Kurup A, eds. *Equity, social determinants and public health programmes.* Geneva, World Health Organization.

Lund HM, Cervero R, Willson RW (2004). *Travel characteristics of transit-oriented development in California. Final report.* Pomona, CA (funded by Caltrans Transportation Grant).

Mace RL. (1998). Universal design in housing. *Assistive Technology*, 10:21–28.

McAliden S et al. (2003). *Economic contribution of the Automotive Industry to the US economy. A study prepared for the Alliance of Automobile Manufacturers – an update.* Ann Arbor, MI, Center for Automotive Research.

Mehndiratta S, Darido G (2011). *Measuring accessibility and initial steps towards using accessibility indicators to drive policy and investment decisions.* Washington DC, World Bank (Transport Forum 2011: 50 Years of Innovation in Transport – Achievements and Future Challenges).

Mendis S, Banerjee A (2010). Cardiovascular disease: equity and social determinants. In: Blas E, Sivasankara Kurup A, eds. *Equity, social determinants and public health programmes.* Geneva, World Health Organization.

Mishra S (2011). *Gender and urban transport: the Mumbai experience.* World Bank, Washington, DC (Transport Forum 2011: 50 Years of Innovation in Transport – Achievements and Future Challenges).

Nantulya V, Reich M (2003). Equity dimensions of road traffic injuries in low- and middle-income countries. *Injury Control and Safety Promotion*, 10:13–20.

Nurul Amin ATM. (2009). *Reducing emissions from private cars: incentive measures for behavioural change.* Nairobi, United Nations Environmental Programme.

NYC-VS (2011). *Health benefits of active transportation in New York City.* New York, NY, New York City Vital Signs, New York City Department of Health and Mental Hygiene (Special Report, 10).

O'Fallon C (2010). *Auditing public transport accessibility in New Zealand.* Wellington, Pinnacle Research & Policy Ltd.

O'Neill MS, Zanobetti A, Schwartz J (2005). Disparities by race in heat-related mortality in four US cities: the role of air conditioning prevalence. *Journal of Urban Health*, 82:191–197.

OECD (2002). *Strategies to reduce greenhouse gas emissions from road transport: analytical methods.* Paris, Organisation for Economic Co-operation and Development.

Ostro B (2004). *Outdoor air pollution.* Geneva, World Health Organization (Environmental Burden of Disease Series No. 5).

PAHO (2009). *Advocating for safe and healthy public transportation.* Washington, DC, Pan-American Health Organization.

PAHO (2010). *Resolution CE146.R4. Non-governmental Organizations in Official Relations with PAHO.* Washington, DC, Pan-American Health Organization.

Patel V et al. (2010). Mental disorders: equity and social determinants. In: Blas E, Sivasankara Kurup A, eds. *Equity, social determinants and public health programmes.* Geneva, World Health Organization.

Peters D (1998). Breadwinners, homemakers and beasts of burden: a gender perspective on transport and mobility. *Sustainable Development International*, 4–7: 1–4.

Pope A et al. (2002). Lung cancer, cardiopulmonary mortality, and long-term exposure to fine particulate air pollution. *JAMA*, 287:1132–1141.

Redlener I (2006). *The growing health care access crisis for American children: one in four at risk.* New York, NY, The Children's Health Fund.

Rice L (2004). *Transportation spending by low-income California households: lessons for the San Francisco Bay area.* San Francisco, CA, Public Policy Institute of California.

Rodrigue J (2008). *Transportation and Economic Development.* London, Routledge (http://people.hofstra.edu/geotrans/eng/ch7en/conc7en/ch7c1en.html, accessed 14 September 2011).

Saffron D (2001). *Targeting young drivers? Need to re-think. Proceedings of the Road Safety Research, Policing and Education Conference, Melbourne, 16–18th September. Vol. 2, pp. 269–275.*

Saldarriaga CA, Vergara CA (2008). *Who switches to gas? A study of a fuel conversion program in Colombia.* Medellin, Colombia, Latin American and Caribbean Environmental Economics Program – LACEEP (Working Paper Series No. 2008-WP6).

Saleh W (2007). Success and failure of travel demand management: Is congestion charging the way forward? *Transportation Research* (Part A)41:611–614.

Salvador E, Reis R, Florindo A (2010). Practice of walking and its association with perceived environment among elderly Brazilians living in a region of low socioeconomic level. *International Journal of Behavioral Nutrition and Phys Activity*, 7:67.

Schafer A et al. (2009). *Transportation in a climate-constrained world.* Cambridge, MA, MIT Press.

Schmidt LA et al. (2010). Alcohol: equity and social determinants. In: Blas E, Sivasankara Kurup A, eds. *Equity, social determinants and public health programmes.* Geneva, World Health Organization.

Son B, Hwang KY (2001). *Seoul experience with congestion pricing. Ninth World Conference on Transportation Research, Seoul, 22–27 July 2001.*

Souza E, Carvalho de Lima ML (2006). *Panorama da violência urbana no Brasil e suas capitais [The panorama of urban violence in Brazil and its capitals]. Ciência & Saúde Coletiva*, 11:363–373.

Spinney J, Scott D, Newbold B (2009). Transport mobility benefits and quality of life: a time-use perspective of elderly Canadians. *Transport Policy*, 16:1–11.

STPP (2003). *Transportation costs and the American dream. Why a lack of transportation choices strains the family budget and hinders home ownership. Special Report.* Washington, DC, Surface Transportation Policy Project.

TBC and IBM (2009). *Future focus: travel.* London, The Telegraph Business Club (White paper, June; http://www-304.ibm.com/businesscenter/cpe/download0/177501/IBM_White_Paper_3.pdf, accessed 30 September 2011).

Tiwari G (2002). Urban transport priorities: meeting the challenge of socio-economic diversity in cities, a case study of Delhi, India. *Cities*, 19:95–103.

Tiwari G (2003). Transport and land-use policies in Delhi. *Bulletin of the World Health Organization*, 81:444–50.

Tiwari G (2005). Self-organizing systems and innovation in Asian Cities. In: Jonson G, Tenstrom E, eds. *Urban transport development: a complex issue.* Berlin and Heidelberg, Springer-Verlag, pp. 144–157.

Tiwari G (2011). Road safety: decade of action with research. *International Journal of Injury Control and Safety Promotion*, 18: 1–2.

Trans-Africa Consortium (2010). *Public Transport in sub-Saharan Africa. Major trends and case studies.* Brussels, UITP – International Association of Public Transport.

UNECE (2001). *Transport AND sustainable development in the ECE region.* New York, NY, United Nations Economic Commission for Europe, Commission on Sustainable Development Ninth Session, 16–27 April 2001 (Background Paper No. 11).

UNEP (2011) *Towards a green economy: pathways to sustainable development and poverty eradication – a synthesis for policy makers.* Nairobi, United Nations Environmental Programme.

UNESCAP, UN-ECLAC & Urban Design Lab (2010). Are we building competitive and liveable cities?: Guidelines on developing ecoefficient and sustainable urban infrastructure in Asia and Latin America. Bangkok, United Nations Economic and Social Commission for Asia and the Pacific.

Valencia A et al. (2009). Los accidentes viales, un grave problema de salud en el Distrito Federal [Road Injuries, a grave health problem in the Federal District]. *Acta Ortopedica Mexicana*, 23:204–208.

Vasconcellos E (2001). *Urban transport, environment, and equity.* Abingdon, United Kingdom, Earthscan.

Vasconcellos E et al. (2010). Seguridad vial y politicas públicas [Road safety and public policies]. In: Galvão LA, Finkelman J, Henao S, eds. *Determinantes ambientales y sociales de la salud [Social and environmental determinants of health].* Mexico, DF, Pan-American Health Organization.

WHO (1997). *World health report: conquering suffering, enriching humanity.* Geneva, World Health Organization.

WHO (2002). Active ageing: a policy framework. Geneva, World Health Organization.

WHO (2004). *World report on road traffic injury prevention.* Geneva, World Health Organization.

WHO (2007a). *Global age-friendly cities: a guide.* Geneva, World Health Organization.

WHO (2007b). *Global report on falls prevention in older age.* Geneva, World Health Organization.

WHO (2008). *Global burden of disease: 2004 update.* Geneva, World Health Organization.

WHO (2009). *Global status report on road safety: time for action.* Geneva, World Health Organization.

WHO (2011a). *World report on disability.* Geneva, World Health Organization.

WHO (2011b). Noncommunicable diseases country profiles 2011. Geneva, World Health Organization.

WHO-EURO (2006). *Health effects and risks of transport systems: the HEARTS project.* Copenhagen, WHO Regional Office for Europe.

WHO-EURO (2007). *Economic assessment of transport infrastructure and policies.* Copenhagen, WHO Regional Office for Europe.

WHO-EURO, EC (2011). *Burden of disease from environmental noise. Quantification of healthy life years lost in Europe.* Copenhagen, WHO Regional Office for Europe-European Commission.

WHO-Government of South Australia (2010). *Adelaide Statement on Health in All Policies.* Adelaide.

Wong CM et al (2008). The effects of air pollution on mortality in socially deprived urban areas in Hong Kong, China. *Environmental Health Perspectives*, 116:1189–1194.

Woodcock J (2009). Public health benefits of strategies to reduce greenhouse-gas emissions: urban land transport. *The Lancet*, 374: 1930–1943.

World Bank (2009). *Strengthening monitoring and evaluation of HIV/AIDS components in road projects.* Washington, DC, Sustainable Development Department, Transport Unit, South Asia Region.

World Bank (2010). *Building an effective knowledge base. The smart road to sustainable transport.* Washington, DC.

World Bank (2011) *Food price watch. Poverty reduction and equity group.* Washington, DC, Poverty Reduction and Economic Management (PREM) Network.

Wright L, Fulton L (2005). Climate change mitigation and transport in developing nations. *Transport Reviews*, 25:691–717.

Wyss K, Kilma P, Laurenz N (2001). The cost of tuberculosis for households and care providers in Dar es Salam, Tanzania. *Tropical Medicine and International Health*, 6:60–68.

NOTES

NOTES